Faith is ultimate knowledge for it is knowing
without knowing,
It is knowledge without knowledge,
It is the fusion of one's soul with the One's

Julian Housman

How lovely are Thy dwellings fair!
O Lord of hosts, how dear
The pleasant tabernacles are
Where Thou dost dwell so near!

John Milton, 1608-1674
from Psalm 84

Thy Dwellings Fair

Churches of Nova Scotia: 1750~1830

Allan F Duffus
G Edward MacFarlane
Elizabeth A Pacey
George W Rogers

LANCELOT PRESS
Hantsport, Nova Scotia

ACKNOWLEDGMENT

This book has been published with the assistance of the Nova Scotia Department of Culture, Recreation and Fitness.

ISBN 0 - 88999 - 166 - 9

Published 1982

Second printing December 1982

Third printing August 1984

LANCELOT PRESS LIMITED, Hantsport, N.S.

ACKNOWLEDGMENTS

The authors have many organizations and individuals to thank. We are grateful for the financial assistance received from the Canada Council and the Province of Nova Scotia, Department of Tourism, which enabled research to be carried out. We would like to thank the staff of the Public Archives of Nova Scotia for their co-operation, and the firm of MacFawn and Rogers Architects for the use of their office resources.

We offer our very special thanks to Mrs. Patricia Hatt for willingly and expertly typing the manuscript, and to Dr. Phyllis Blakeley and Dr. Philip Pacey for reading the manuscript. We also extend thanks to Mr. Barry Johns who contributed to the initial research, and Mr. Ron Wallace who was very helpful in procuring the provincial research grant.

A great many people have provided valuable information and assistance on the individual churches. We sincerely thank the following persons for their help: Mr. Cyril Read (St. John's, Lunenburg), Rev. M. J. Findlay (St. George's, Sydney), Mrs. Marion Woodland (Old St. Edward's, Clementsport), Father Langley MacLean (St. Mary's, Auburn), Rev. R. A. Neish (Christ Church, Karsdale), Rev. D. D. M. Sharp (Old Holy Trinity, Middleton), Mr. H. D. Naugler (St. John's, Cornwallis), Mrs. Franklyn Thompson and Ms. Pat Townsend (Goat Island Baptist Church), Mr. W. E. Brown (All Saints', Granville Centre), Rev. C. R. H. Nixon (St. Luke's, Annapolis Royal), Mr. Duncan Spidell and Rev. J. E. Boyd (North West Range Meeting House), Mr. Harry Gray (Christ Church, Dartmouth), Mrs. Rosemary Eaton and Mrs. Margaret Campbell (Cole Harbour Meeting House), Mrs. Robert Lawrence Fraser and Mr. Eric Pace (William Black Memorial, Glen Margaret), Mr. Don Macgillivray and Dr. Robert Morgan (St. Patrick's, Sydney), and Mrs. Burtus Crouse (St. John's, Sackville). We would also like to gratefully acknowledge the work of the Rev. Dr. M. Allen Gibson, whose extensive series of articles *Churches by the Sea* has been singularly helpful to our project.

CONTENTS

INTRODUCTION

Long before Confederation, when most of Canada was still a wilderness, there were distinctive styles of architecture in Nova Scotia. One of the most important structures in every community, and one of the most characteristic in design, was the local church. As an integral part of early life in Nova Scotia, church buildings reflected the social patterns and spiritual aspirations of the new inhabitants. Perhaps no other building type has recorded the social history of the province as well as the early churches. It is to the credit of the original builders and ensuing congregations that many of their churches still remain.

It is the purpose of this book to record a representative sample of the churches from Nova Scotia's early building period. It is to be hoped that Nova Scotia's oldest churches will be more widely recognized for their provincial, and indeed national, historic and architectural importance. In gathering material for this book, it was decided to focus on the architectural as well as the historical aspects of the individual church buildings. Information on design influences and early construction methods has also been included, so that the reader might appreciate why certain designs were used, and how they were implemented by the early settlers.

By way of introduction, this work begins with a brief overview of the early establishment of the various denominations in the province.

Catholic Beginnings

As early as 1504, European fishermen began to work along the coast of Nova Scotia. While they made no permanent settlements during the 16th century, they often returned repeatedly to the same place along the shore to stop and dry their catch. Between 1520 and 1525, the Portuguese came each summer to a beautiful bay, known later to the French as "Baie des Espagnols" and today, as Sydney Harbour. Another popular fishing ground was Canso, where the first Jesuit missionaries set foot in Canada in May, 1611. Those missionaries, Father Pierre Biard and his assistant Father Ennemond Massé were on their way from France to the French settlement at Port Royal when they stopped to celebrate mass at Canso.

In 1605, Pierre du Gast, Sieur de Monts, had founded Port Royal, the earliest permanent settlement in Canada. De Monts, himself a Huguenot, had brought with him two priests and two Huguenot ministers; religious controversy, akin to that of the homeland, flared up. By 1610, King Henry IV had recalled Sieur de Monts and appointed Jean de Biencourt, Sieur de Poutrincourt, as the new Governor of Port Royal. The French king also had stipulated that Sieur de Poutrincourt must have Jesuit missionaries to minister to the settlers and convert the Indians; hence the arrival of Fathers Biard and Massé.

As Acadian settlements were established in the province, other missionary priests were sent to Nova Scotia from France and Quebec. After 1659, Nova Scotia was part of the new diocese of Quebec which included all French possessions in North America. Accordingly, the Seminary of Quebec, founded in 1663, and the Seminary of Saint-Sulpice, founded at Montreal in 1677, sent many missionaries to Nova Scotia. The priests had a powerful influence over the Micmac Indians whom they treated as friends and allies rather than as a conquered people.

The French Catholic missionaries were the first to construct chapels, which were often extremely primitive. For example, in 1616, at Port Royal, Father Huel celebrated mass in a "cabane d'écorce"; this structure would probably have been constructed of logs sharpened at both ends and driven side-by-side into the ground to form a palisade. The roof would have been formed of branches covered with bark, and the cracks between the logs caulked with clay. The building of permanent church structures was, undoubtedly, hampered by the French-English political strife. Port Royal was captured 14 times. Also, in 1755, the Acadians were expelled from Nova Scotia for their refusal, on religious grounds, to swear allegiance to the British king. As a result, none of the early French Catholic chapels survived.

The Royal Chapel of Saint-Louis at the Fortress of Louisbourg was the antithesis of the primitive missionary chapels. This Royal Chapel, which also served as a parish church, was embellished with gilt-trimmed plasterwork, and outfitted with furnishings from France. And though it was as fine as any chapel in a French chateau, it did not survive the capture and destruction of Louisbourg. Recently, the Chapelle Saint-Louis has been re-created by Parks Canada as part of the reconstruction of the fortress and town of Louisbourg.

With the founding of Halifax in 1749, a number of English-speaking Roman Catholics, predominantly Irish, settled in Halifax. These Catholics, along with any others in the province, were prevented, by various statutes, from owning land, building churches and worshipping in public. When these restrictions were lifted in 1784, Catholic churches began to appear. Unfortunately today, very few Catholic churches remain from Georgian times. This is largely because the Catholic Church, more than any other denomination, has been prone to periodically replacing old churches with newer ones, leaving the fund of historic structures seriously depleted.

The Established Church and Its Dependents

The history of the Anglicans in Nova Scotia is different from that of the Roman Catholics or of any of the other Protestant denominations. The leading settlers that came from England to found the garrison towns like Halifax and Annapolis Royal were primarily members of the Church of England. Thus, it is not surprising that the first Assembly at Halifax passed an act in 1758 which made the Church of England the established or official church of Nova Scotia. Because of its elevated status, the Church of England received support from the Governor and Council in the form of grants of land and public money for the building of churches.

Another important factor in determining the growth of the Church of England in Nova Scotia was the help given by the Society for the Propagation of the Gospel in Foreign Parts. This productive English society not only sent out many missionaries and schoolmasters to the province but financially supported almost every Anglican clergyman throughout the 18th and well into the 19th centuries.

The coming of the United Empire Loyalists, after the American Revolution, gave a great impetus to the growth of the Church of England. Many of 28,000 Loyalists who came to the Maritime Provinces were Episcopalian or Anglican. A number of distinguished clergymen accompanied the exiles to Nova Scotia. These included Jacob Bailey, Bernard Michael Howseal, John Wiswall and the Rev. Dr. Charles Inglis who was consecrated as the first Bishop of Nova Scotia in 1787.

Clearly, the resources, in terms of land, monetary grants and available clergy, made it possible for the Anglicans to gather congregations together and build churches for them. The largest number of Nova Scotia's earliest churches are Anglican. It is fortunate that past generations of Anglican congregations have maintained these historic churches for present and future generations to appreciate.

The story of the "foreign protestants" is closely linked to that of the Church of England. In order to colonize their lands in Nova Scotia, the British government recruited settlers from France, Germany and Switzerland. Some 3,000 foreign protestant settlers arrived at Halifax between 1750 and 1752; in June, 1753, the majority set off to found Lunenburg leaving behind about 25 families in Halifax. Many but not all of these settlers, who were of Lutheran and Calvinistic backgrounds, were absorbed into the Anglican Church which ministered to them. In Halifax, the small group of remaining foreign settlers formed a separate congregation but followed the Church of England doctrines. In Lunenburg, the foreign protestants worshipped as Anglicans though the services were delivered in French and German; a division finally occurred in 1769, when a significant number of the settlers formed their own separate Lutheran church.

The Dissenters

Between 1760 and 1776, a great number of New England settlers, approximately 12,000 strong, migrated to Nova Scotia. They were, for the most part, Congregationalists. During the 1760's, the Congregationalists formed the largest denomination, numerically speaking, in the province. They built "meeting houses", a very distinctive form of church design which had a lasting effect on early church architecture in Nova Scotia. But the ascendency of Congregationalism was short-lived. When the American Revolution broke out, many of the Congregationalist settlers sympathized with the rebels and their ministers, and some returned to New England. And of those that stayed, a substantial number were absorbed later into the Baptist or Presbyterian denominations.

In fact, the success of the early revival movement known as the "New Light" movement contributed further to the decline of the Congregational church. The first great preacher of the "New Lights" in Nova Scotia was Henry Alline. Born at Newport, Rhode Island, in 1748, Alline emigrated to Falmouth, Nova Scotia, in 1760. He travelled throughout the Maritimes, preaching the new brand of Calvinism with fervid eloquence. Several "New Light" congregations were established by Alline and eventually became Baptist congregations. Gradually, through the work of Alline's disciples, the Baptist denomination gained many of the most influential families of New England origin, and became one of the most important denominations in the province.

Today, a number of interesting, old Baptist meeting houses are still in existence.

The first Presbyterian ministers in Nova Scotia were the Huguenot missionaries who accompanied Sieur de Monts and his colonists to Port Royal in 1605. However,

Presbyterianism did not begin to gain a foothold in the province until the latter half of the 18th century. Some of the New England Congregationalists who stayed in Nova Scotia after the American Revolution eventually became part of the Presbyterian denomination. Thus, one finds the Rev. James Murdoch, a Presbyterian clergyman, ministering, in 1767, to a flock of predominantly Congregationalist settlers at Grand Pré. For many years, Murdoch also conducted extensive missionary work in the area and as far afield as Amherst.

The great influx of Scottish settlers to Pictou County, beginning with the arrival of the ship *Hector* in 1773, made the Presbyterians the most numerous denomination in the province in 1867. A large number of old Presbyterian churches are to be found in Nova Scotia, but because the denomination was slightly later in establishing its congregations, there are only a few churches that remain from the earliest building period.

The Methodists, or Wesleyan Methodists as they were called, gained a few converts among the New England settlers, but generally Methodists were people who had emigrated from England. The chief spokesman and pioneer missionary was William Black, who like Henry Alline, preached in most of the villages of Nova Scotia and New Brunswick. The largest concentration of Methodists in Nova Scotia was in Cumberland County where a significant number of Yorkshire families, including Black's own family, had settled between 1770 and 1775. Methodism was, however, slow to grow, so that in 1800, there were only five such ministers in all the Maritime Provinces. The number of historic Methodist church buildings, therefore, reflects the slow growth of the denomination in its early years.

Thus, the various religious denominations had established themselves in the new colony of Nova Scotia. By the time of the first, official Canadian census, completed in 1871, there was evidence that some denominations had flourished more than others. For example, there were 103,539 Presbyterians, 102,001 Roman Catholics, 73,430 Baptists, 55,430 Anglicans, 38,683 Methodists and 2,538 Congregationalists. A considerable number of churches had been constructed. Those churches that remain are the tangible reminders of the hardships and devotion of the missionaries and settlers of early Nova Scotia.

DESIGN INFLUENCES

Even a cursory look at Canadian architecture will reveal areas in Canada where there is a distinctive architectural style. Found primarily in regions of early settlements, this distinctive architecture was the result of early settlers bringing building traditions with them, and adapting the traditions of the homeland to the conditions of the new land. In some cases, the original building type survived for generations with little change; in other cases, the buildings were modified to suit a different way of life.

In Quebec, the style of the early French Canadian house is unique to that area, with its steeply pitched, bell-shaped roof and heavy masonry walls. The influence of the church is evident everywhere, particularly in the small towns along the St. Lawrence River where the dominant feature is the silhouette of the great, parish church.

In the same way, there is a distinctive, early, regional architecture in the Maritime Provinces, particularly in Nova Scotia. An interplay of historical events in Nova Scotia resulted in a truly indigenous architecture. The two most significant events were the coming of settlers from the Thirteen Colonies in the latter half of the 18th century, and the importation of classicism by the British at about the same time. As part of the British contribution, the Scottish brought, particularly to the Pictou area, traditions of building in stone. The greatest legacy of the American migrations is generally in that area west of the line from Halifax to Truro. British classicism in its pure form is found primarily in Halifax.

The greatest concentration of significant early architecture in Nova Scotia, therefore, is in the Annapolis Valley, the Minas Basin area, the Pictou area, the shoreline from Yarmouth to Halifax and the city of Halifax itself.

Although French settlers preceeded both those from the Thirteen Colonies and Britain, their early buildings are not seen today. When the Acadians were expelled by the British in 1755, their lands were given to others and their houses and barns burned. Thus their tradition of local building was lost. However, two modern-day reconstructions of French buildings are the Habitation at Port Royal and the Fortress and town at Louisbourg.

Thus, the roots of Nova Scotian architecture originated in the American colonies and Britain. For example, a New Englander in Nova Scotia would construct his building as his forefathers had done in the American colonies. The British government, in Halifax, would construct buildings according to the established rules of classicism practised in Britain. Examples of these early building styles remain, but as time went on, there was an eventual blending of the two styles which resulted in an architecture which is unique in Canada.

The American Influence

Following the expulsion of the Acadians in 1755, the British government opened the way for thousands of New Englanders to settle in Nova Scotia in the 1760's. Farmers from New England came to the rich farmlands of the Annapolis Valley and Minas Basin area. Fishermen settled in the communities of Yarmouth, Barrington, Liverpool, and Chester. Merchants and tradesmen came to Halifax. It is estimated, that between 1760 and 1776, approximately 12,000 New Englanders, or "planters" as they were called, came to Nova Scotia. These New Englanders saw Nova Scotia as an opportunity to obtain good farmland, as similar land at home was becoming scarce. Even though Nova Scotia was some distance away, these early settlers considered Nova Scotia an extension of New England.

Later, in the 1780's, following the American Revolution, a second migration came to Nova Scotia. These people, known as United Empire Loyalists, wished to remain loyal to the Crown, and came from the Thirteen Colonies for refuge in Nova Scotia; others went to Ontario and New Brunswick. Approximately 10,000 Loyalists came from New York and settled at Shelburne, Nova Scotia. The Loyalists were a more sophisticated and educated group than the New England Planters. This is evident by the many large houses they built, and businesses they established. They were also responsible for educational centres such as Kings College in Windsor.

As the various New Englanders and families from the rest of the Thirteen Colonies settled in Nova Scotia, they brought with them traditions that eventually became firmly established in their new homeland. The character of buildings in Nova Scotia today is the result of these traditions.

Generally, the building material for early American churches was determined largely by geography and geology, whereas the style was determined by denomination. The extensive use of wood is probably the most identifiable characteristic of early American architecture, and hence early Nova Scotian architecture. This is natural, considering the availability of the material and the ease with which it is worked.

In America, carpenters and skilled workmen were plentiful and the woodworking trade had developed to a high level. For instance, New Englanders were shipping furniture and pre-fabricated structures to Barbados, Jamaica, and even Nova Scotia. In fact, when the New England troops arrived at Grand Pré to fight the French in 1710, they brought with them "materials for two block houses". When the New England Planters arrived to settle in pre-Loyalist Nova Scotia, they brought with them not only tools and cherished pieces of furniture, but also pre-cut and hewn timbers to build their new homes.

The early New England building was a geometric form, almost totally without ornamentation except perhaps around the entrance. Windows were regularly spaced and exterior walls were finished with narrow clapboard siding. The roof was pitched with little overhang, and was intersected by one or more large chimneys. Most often the building stood alone, as one in a composition with other buildings. Thus, the farmhouse was an independent structure from the tool shed, which in turn stood apart from the barn, and so on.

The Meeting House

The meeting house style was brought to Nova Scotia between 1760 and 1776 from New England as a creation of the Congregationalists. There were no European precedents for this type of building. It originated in the American colonies as a community building where the business of the town was conducted and, at appropriate times during the week, religious services held. Built first by the Puritans in New England, it was without ornamentation, embellishment or symbols that might recall the Church of England.

Although the American Puritan was a democrat at heart, and everybody had a vote, seats in the meeting house were usually assigned by a committee of the town on the basis of class distinction. Furthermore, whenever a new meeting house was proposed for a town, everyone wanted the building to be as close as possible to his or her home, because of the poor roads and the possibility of attack from Indians. This often led to bitter disagreements within the community; on occasion an arbitrator from another town would be called upon to decide the site for the structure.

Comforts in the early meeting house were sparse. Often the minister wore his coat and gloves as he delivered the sermon. Water often turned to ice in the baptismal font, and the communion bread froze solid.

The first type of meeting house was square, or nearly square, in plan, with entrances generally on three sides. The pulpit was located on the fourth side. The roof rose from the four walls in a pyramidal shape and was sometimes capped by a cupola or belfry. There is no record that meeting houses of this type were ever built in Nova Scotia.

Early in the 18th century, the meeting house evolved from a square plan to a rectangular plan with a pitched, gabled roof. If desired, a bell tower was placed at one end of the structure. The main entrance was usually in the centre of one long side, and sometimes there were doors at the two ends as well. On the interior, the pulpit was placed opposite the main entrance door, and a gallery ran around the three remaining walls. This style of meeting house, barn-like in its simplicity, and very much like a house, rather than a church in form, was built in Nova Scotia. The meeting house at Barrington, constructed in 1765 by settlers from Cape Cod, is an example. In this

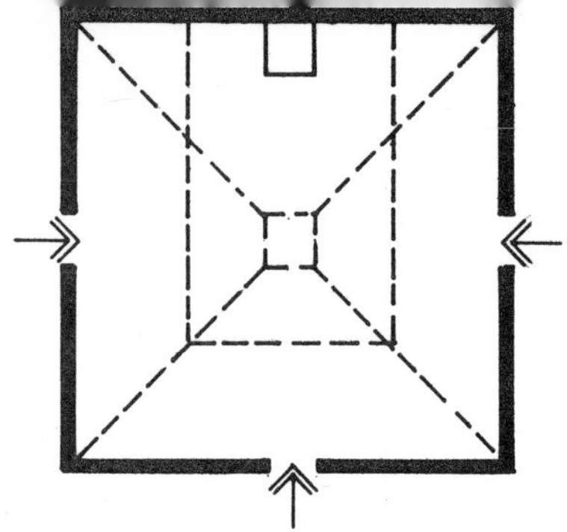

Early 1700's

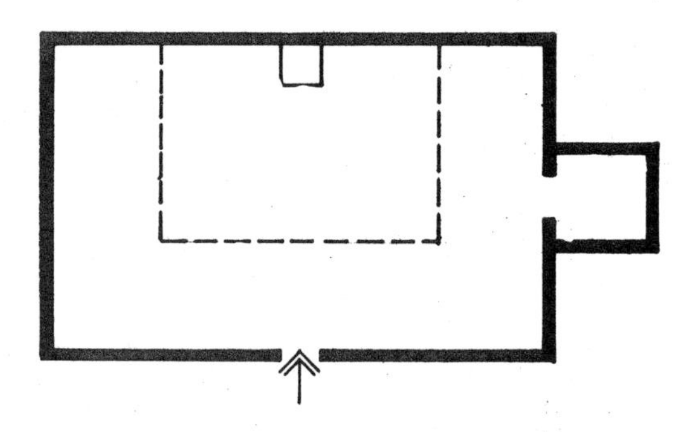

ca. 1730-1800

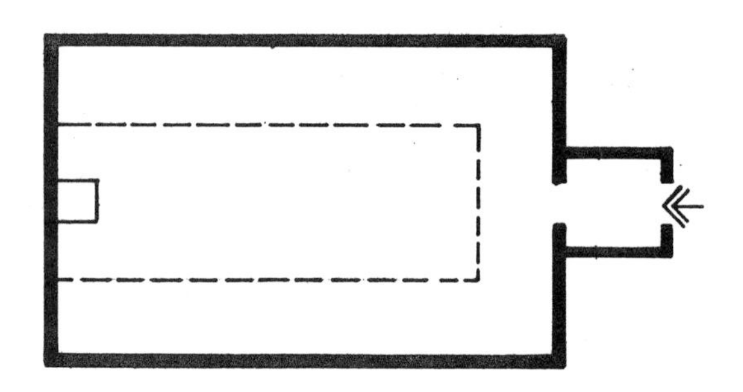

After 1800

case, there was no bell tower. A later example, the Covenanter Church at Grand Pré, does have a bell tower attached at one end.

The evolution to the oblong plan had been due to the limitations in spanning the roof space of the original square type of meeting house. Finally, the meeting house became a place solely for religious purposes. Thus, its form became more similar to traditional church buildings. The entrance was usually at the west end, rather than on one of the long sides. The roof became more gently sloped, and the building more highly ornamented. The pulpit was placed at the opposite end to the main entrance, with the gallery around the three remaining walls. The transition of the meeting house to this style occurred about 1810 in Nova Scotia.

The meeting house at North West Range, built in 1818, is typical of this third style of meeting house. The Goat Island Baptist Church of 1810, is also a good example, though it has slight variations, such as a single gallery at one end rather than galleries on three sides. The Goat Island Church also has a steeple which was added somewhat later.

Although the meeting house originated with the Congregationalists, its plan was easily adaptable, and other denominations adopted it for their own use. The Baptists, Presbyterians and Methodists built meeting houses for worship in pioneer Nova Scotia.

British Classicism

British classical or Georgian architecture came to Canada in 1749 with the founding of Halifax. Classicism was the style of architecture adopted by Britain both for use at home and abroad, and was characterized by the strength and solidity that typified the image of the emerging British empire. It was the perfect expression of confidence and power.

British architects relied heavily on the Italian Renaissance for inspiration, and were influenced by the writings of Italian Renaissance architects, particularly Andrea Palladio and his *Four Books of Architecture.*

Palladio was born in Padua in 1508, and originally trained as a sculptor and stone mason. He was influenced by the writings of the Roman architect, Vitruvius, author of the only architectural book preserved from the Roman and Greek worlds. Palladio's *Four Books of Architecture,* first published in Venice in 1570, dealt with building materials, building techniques, the orders of architecture, such as Ionic, Doric, or Corinthian, and villas, civic works, and Roman temples. Palladio was the leading exponent of the re-birth of early Roman and Greek classical architecture in the 16th century. He illustrated methods for designing correct proportions for the various parts of a building, all, of course, in the classical style.

In England, it was Inigo Jones who first imported Palladianism. Jones visited Italy in 1614, and acquired a number of Palladio's original drawings, and a copy of the *Four Books of Architecture.* The Palladian influence is evident in Jones' design of the Banqueting House at Whitehall, and at the Queen's House in Greenwich. The first complete English translation of the *Four Books of Architecture* was not published until 1715; afterwards, Palladianism became a ruling style in England.

Other British architects influenced architecture in North America. Notably, Sir Christopher Wren set the style for church design. Wren was the architect in charge of rebuilding London, following the Great Fire of London in 1666. He was as much a mathematician and scientist as an architect, and his design for the dome of St. Paul's Cathedral in London, demonstrates a high degree of structural ingenuity. He prepared a master plan for the rebuilding of London which included the re-design of a number of small parish churches. The master plan was not carried out, but Wren did succeed in designing fifty-eight London churches. The most striking feature about these churches, invariably, is the tower. Talbot Hamlin, in his compendious work, *Architecture Through the Ages,* commented on Wren's magnificent church steeples. "For these churches, accordingly, Wren designed a series of extremely varied towers. They usually start as simple rectangular masses, often topped with a stage decorated with orders. This carries in turn an element that is either octagonal or circular, above which is the spire proper. The octagonal or circular element may itself be in several decreasing stages."

James Gibbs, a Scot, was a pupil of Sir Christopher Wren. In 1728, Gibbs wrote his *Book of Architecture*, followed in 1733, by *Rules for Drawing the Several Parts of Architecture*. These books were perhaps the most important single means by which British classical architecture was transmitted to North America. Gibbs gave precise details and specifications for several of his buildings, including the Church of Saint Martin-in-the-Fields, London, constructed between 1721 and 1726.

In Nova Scotia, buildings built entirely in the British classical tradition are to be found mainly in Halifax, although the influence of British classicism did reach rural areas in terms of architectural details or embellishments. Pure British classicism was confined to major important structures such as Province House, and Government House in Halifax. However, the British style of classical architecture influenced building in Nova Scotia until well into the 1800's.

Probably the purest example of imported British classical architecture in Nova Scotia is Province House. Completed in 1819, it is typical of British administrative architecture, and set a high standard for legislative buildings in Canada. The building is constructed of stone, with classical pediments, niches and columns, and conveys a sense of dignity and permanence which were symbolic of British power and stability.

The Nova Scotia Style

Although there are "pure" examples of American architecture and "pure" examples of British classical architecture in Nova Scotia, the essence of Nova Scotian architecture is a synthesis of the two styles. A typical building would be simply and sturdily constructed of wood, sheathed in narrow clapboarding, and capped by a pitched roof, all reminiscent of the colonial tradition. There would invariably be, however, elements or details of British classical architecture at the door, windows, and along the roof eaves. These classical elements would be adapted to wood, and scaled to the size of the particular building.

St. Mary's Church in Auburn is typical. Its simple, rectangular form constructed in wood recalls the New England meeting house. The builders then superimposed elements of British classicism on the basic form of the church by incorporating into the design classical pediments and capitals, a Palladian window, and a fine Wren-style steeple. These classical details executed in wood and integrated with the New England vernacular form resulted in a building which is exceedingly tasteful in design, and indigenous in style to Nova Scotia.

A few of the early churches were built with gothic door or window arches. These gothic arches are an anomaly in the otherwise classical detailing.

Because buildings in the Nova Scotian style are neither a complete replication of the American type, nor fully representative of the British style, but rather a mix of the two, they constitute an architecture which is unique in Canada.

EARLY CONSTRUCTION

By the middle and late eighteenth century, nearly all building in England and Scotland was carried out in stone, as timber was in very short supply. However, in Nova Scotia, as elsewhere in colonial North America, the techniques of medieval timber framing had been adapted by the settlers to meet the needs of the new world, and to enable better utilization of the different species of wood which abounded in the forests.

Wood Construction

The techniques of early timber frame building in Nova Scotia, as it applied to churches, were either adapted from previous experience with houses and barns in the area, or were imported from other colonies. The problem in designing a timber frame for a church or meeting house, as opposed to a residence, was the increase in "loading" on the structure from the weight of the congregation. To add to this, the space in a church had to provide clear vision to the pulpit which meant that interior walls and posts, with complex bracing, had to be avoided. This was solved by the use of roof trusses pegged to the main timber frame. In the case of those churches with galleries, the support columns would have some bracing effect but not so much as to be disruptive visually. As well, the pews were built in such a way as to force the congregation to face the pulpit or altar.

The term "timber frame construction" means the use of heavy timbers, either sawn or axed square, which were spaced evenly according to the length and width of the church. The sills of the frame sat on a stone foundation, built-up with boulders and stones from the fields nearby. The sills were notched to receive floor joists and uprights for the wall framing. The corner posts were attached at the top by girts or plates into which were fitted the rafters or roof trusses depending on the size of the church. The earliest construction using rafters did so without a ridge board. Purlins were notched into the rafters instead. The connection between any two framing members would be made by a mortise and tenon joint and pinned with a wooden peg.

Firstly, the frames would be cut on the ground, and corresponding members often marked with Roman numerals before being assembled. Primary frames would also be erected for the galleries, and temporarily braced until the lighter floor joists were in place, and the whole assembly made stable.

The roof would be next, followed by exterior finish or roof shingles. The exterior cladding would be overlapping clapboards or shingles depending on the geographical areas. The width of clapboard left exposed to weather, a matter of experience and local tradition, varied from less than four inches on buildings in unprotected coastal areas, to almost six inches on buildings inland. The earliest protection to the exterior of the churches in Nova Scotia was a coat of lime whitewash. This was applied every spring to keep the crawling beetles and bugs away, and to condition the wood for the dryness of summer air. When paint became the common material, it was generally the type used on boats in the coastal communities. Its toughness and ability to withstand much of the effects of weathering is the reason for the excellent condition of some of Nova Scotia's oldest churches.

Additional structures to the original building were generally framed up separately, and either pegged in, or bolted to, the main church. The tower at the Covenanter Church was framed separately and attached to the body of the structure. As well, some of the chancel additions to the other churches were added in this manner.

Heavy timber framing can be readily seen in the roof spaces and tower structures of many of the churches discussed in this work, including Old Holy Trinity at Middleton, Old St. Edward's at Clementsport and Goat Island Baptist Church.

In order to keep out drafts, the builders often filled the space between the outer and inner walls with an insulating material. This could have been brick, wood chips, or, in some cases, seaweed. At St. Paul's in Halifax, for example, brick nogging was used in the wall space. To further cut down drafts, birch bark was used as an air barrier, applied completely to the exterior wall sheathing before the clapboards were nailed in place.

Interior walls were usually finished with plaster on lath. Plaster lime was sometimes imported from New Brunswick. The pioneers also made their own plaster lime by crushing and burning clam and quahog shells which were easily available on the beaches. The plaster was stiffened by the addition of hay or hair to the lime mixture. By the early 19th century, a supply of high-quality gypsum was discovered in Cape Breton, and a fine, white lime plaster was developed.

The frames for early buildings, houses, barns and churches alike, were erected by muscle power alone. Thus, there developed a kind of mutual assistance program in each community whenever a new building was required. This meant the opportunity for a social occasion, and gave rise to the famous

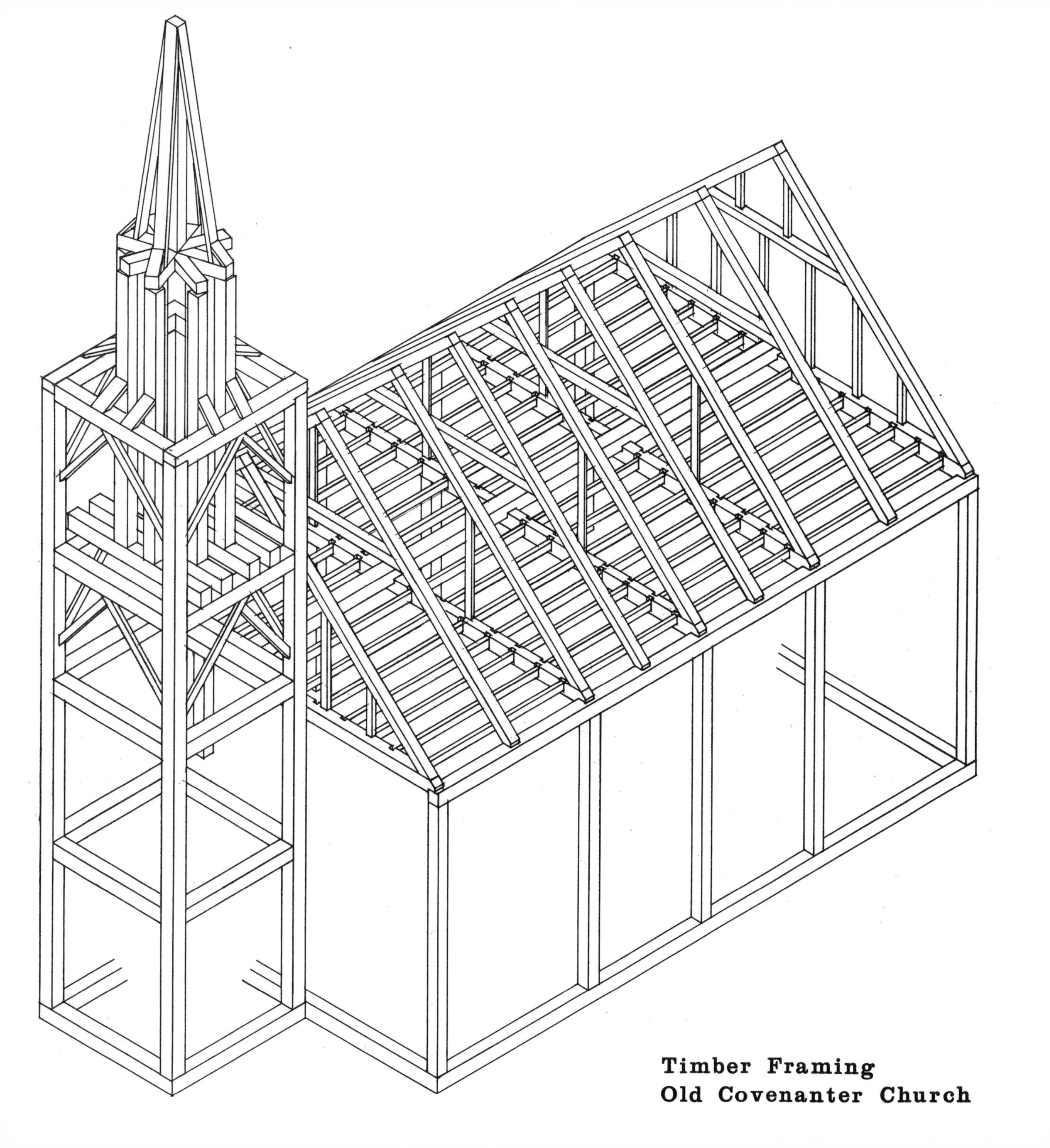
Timber Framing
Old Covenanter Church

pioneer raising "bee".

In some cases, building materials or complete building frames were brought from elsewhere. For instance, the frame for St. Paul's in Halifax was imported from Boston, and doors and windows for St. Mary's in Auburn were brought, pre-made, from Halifax.

Pit-sawing was a common technique in New England for sawing planks from logs. The log was laid over a pit and sawn by two men, the "sawyer" standing on the log, and the "pitman" in the pit. Early sawmills in Canada were neither very efficient nor very fast. It was some time before they replaced skilled axemen and pit sawyers completely.

When Halifax was founded in 1749, the English built a water-powered sawmill across the harbour. And later, when the Loyalists came to settle in Nova Scotia, the government built sawmills near their communities to provide lumber for their building projects. In the Maritimes, sawmills were often worked by tidal power using water trapped behind the dam after the fall of the tide. Such mills could be found in the Bay of Fundy area as early as 1800. By the latter half of the 19th century, most lumber was cut in sawmills. The development of the steam engine, and its use in the sawmill, produced lumber more quickly and efficiently than could be done by hand-cutting. Characteristically early sawn lumber produced wide boards up to two feet or more in width for walls and floors.

The woods of Nova Scotia provided much in the way of building material to please the builder. There were pines, oaks, firs and poplars of varying hardness and strength, which enabled the builder to choose the most appropriate type of wood. The tradition and experience of the carpenter, as well as skill, were factors in the choice, but generally it was understood that certain wood was used for specific parts of the construction. The sills were most often tamarack or white oak, with the rest of the framing being of red pine or white oak. Red pine was normally used for rafters, purlins and roof boards, as red pine contains a good amount of resin to act as a preservative. Roof shingles and horizontal or clapboard siding were of Eastern white cedar, red pine or white oak. Balsam fir, tamarack and hemlock were common flooring wood, while white oak or white pine was used for general finish work and detailing. Sugar or hard maple and other woods, such as butternut and ash, were used for furniture, pews and pulpit pieces.

Builders and Tools

Few records exist as to the names and trades of the actual builders of the early churches of Nova Scotia. There has been a long-standing belief that many churches were built by ships' carpenters which may account for some of the unusual construction methods. For example, huge, sturdy, "ship's knees" were

used in the construction of the Barrington Meeting House and the Goat Island Baptist Church.

However, when the Loyalists came to Nova Scotia, many carpenters and joiners were among them. The carpenter was thoroughly familiar with all aspects of the craft of building. The joiner was a skilled furniture maker and would do up such things as panelling, altar pieces and pews for churches. In some cases, the exterior decoration or detail was done by a joiner. As well as these tradesmen, it should be noted that, in some communities, there were, undoubtedly, farmers and woodsmen who were not afraid to undertake the framing up and raising of a church or meeting house, leaving the finish and details to be carried out by a carpenter or joiner.

An eyewitness account describes the building of two Presbyterian meeting houses in Pictou County in July, 1787. "During this month the men were chiefly engaged in building the two meeting houses; but, instead of employing contractors to build them, they agreed to divide the work into a number of lots, and appointed a party of themselves to every lot. One party cut the logs and hauled them to the site; another hewed them and laid them in their place; a third provided boards for the roof and floors; a fourth provided the shingles; those who were joiners were appointed to make the doors and windows, and those who did not care to work provided the glass and nails. Moss was stuffed between the logs to keep out the wind and rain; but neither was one of them seated otherwise than by logs laid where seats should be. Public worship was conducted in the open air all this summer, and part of harvest, till the churches were finished, and we had the same kind Providence preserving us from wind and rain and tempest as we had last year; but no sooner were the houses built than great rain came on the Sabbath. Such were the first two churches of Pictou, and for a while they had no pulpits, purely because they could make a shift without them, and when they were made, they were not of mahogany but of the white pine of Pictou."

The early settlers of Nova Scotia placed great value on tools, and the ability to use them. Each Loyalist male over the age of fourteen was issued a felling axe upon arrival in Nova Scotia. Each pioneer family was issued with simple building tools that could be used for the rough framing of an essential shelter. The carpenter, however, had a selection of tools which were divided into two categories: splitting tools and cutting tools. Within these two categories, tools were then classified according to whether they were used for heavy framing and rough work or for finishing and detail work. Each carpenter built up his stock of tools, some of which he would make himself from the time of his apprenticeship, starting with the tools for rough and heavy work. The tools for heavy framing, with which the early churches in Nova Scotia were built, include axes, saws, mallets, augers and planes.

The broad axe, the most essential tool in early Nova Scotia, was used to square logs into usuable structural pieces. The broad axe was sharpened only along one side, and when used, left a smooth surface with slight intersecting marks from each cut. The handle, usually made from maple, was reversible for left or right-handed use.

There were two types of adze used in early Nova Scotia: the carpenter's adze and that of the shipwright, which were distinguishable by the poll. The carpenter's adze had a flat heavy poll while that of the shipwright had an elongated tapered spike. The adze had its cutting edge set perpendicular to the handle, and like the broad axe, was sharpened on one side only. The marks of the broad axe and adze are often confused at first glance. The adze leaves shallow curved depressions with some minor ridging along the length of the timber, the overall effect varying from a slight ripple to almost complete smoothness.

The gimlet was a ships' carpenter's tool developed in England and used to make holes for screws. The gimlet cuts the wood fibers as opposed to forcing them apart. The mark of the gimlet hole is a rough taper on the side, and a screw thread at the lowest part of the hole.

Awls and augers are hole makers, with handles that one man could turn fairly easily. Each had a pointed end and sharp corners to chip away twisted wood, as the hole was made by twisting the wood fibres apart. Some augers were heated until the point was hot enough to burn its way into the wood. There are various types and sizes of awls and augers, but the markings left in the wood are almost the same; screw-tipped augers leave a groove down the side and a pilot hole in the bottom, while others leave no pilot hole. There, of course, would be some charred markings if the auger were heated.

Mallets were used for two main purposes in early building. The mallet was used as a direct implement for banging together heavy mortise and tenon joints, and "pegging"; it was also used in conjuction with chisels, gouges and the froe. The froe was a wrought-iron knife-type blade with a handle perpendicular to the blade, so that wood could be forced apart after the back of the blade had been driven into it. The froe and mallet together formed a splitting tool essential in making shingles, laths, staves and clapboards.

Most planes were finishing tools, but the heavy plough and tongue plane was used in making wide boards that fit together, such as tongue and groove flooring. This plane was heavy, and more than three feet long; it required two men to work it. The plane had handles on the side of the body and, at the toe, a ring was attached through which a rope could be fastened enabling a third person to pull it. This plane, like the smaller finishing models, had an adjustable fence for cutting grooves along the edge of boards. Tongue and groove boarding is found as flooring in some of the churches discussed in this work.

Pit sawing, and later sawmills, produced the wide boards, for heavy construction. Some of these boards could be converted, by plane, for clapboards, or, by crosscut saws, to the appropriate size for framing doors and windows. The two-man crosscut saw was generally used on large, square timbers, but for smaller work, the frame and bow saws were used. These saws are the forerunners of the band saw. The advantage of these saws was that the blade could be adjusted relative to the frame, to enable cutting along curves and into awkward corners. The frame saw and bow saw were differentiated by whether the blade was on the outside or inside of the wooden frame; the bow saw had its blade outside the frame. The marks of these saws are almost straight, not quite parallel and follow a fairly tight curve; they are most noticeable on the edges of door and window frames.

The finishing tools, used to finish the

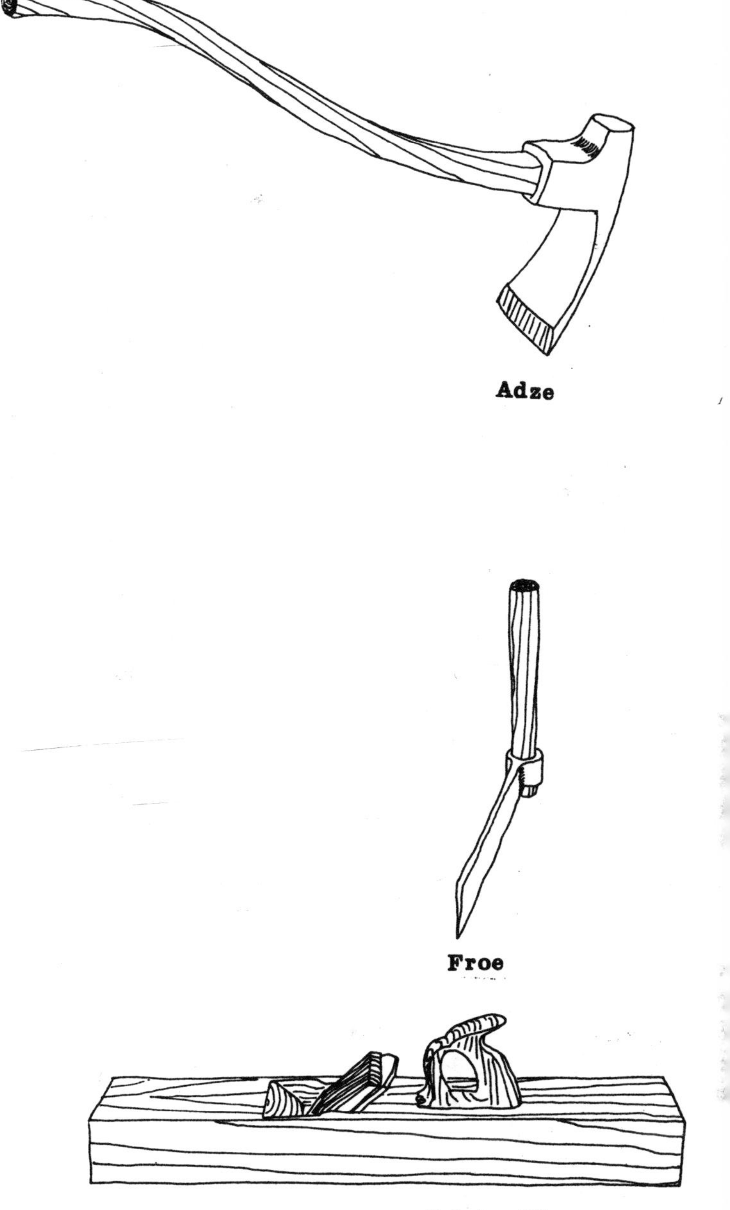
Adze

Froe

Jointer Plane

clapboard siding, frame and set doors and windows, and do any of the detail decoration, were kept separate from the heavy framing tools. The minimum in the finishing tool box was: a brace with a variety of bits, handsaws for rough and fine cutting, a range of chisels and gouges for fitting and carving, marking gauges and squares, and most important of all, a wide selection of planes. The plane was considered to be the ultimate finishing tool. There were many variations from the common plough and tongue smoothing planes, to an unlimited range of moulding planes. The detailed work in the interiors of the churches is physical evidence that the skills were developed to a high standard.

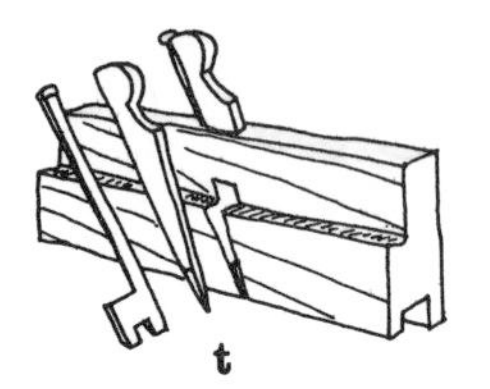

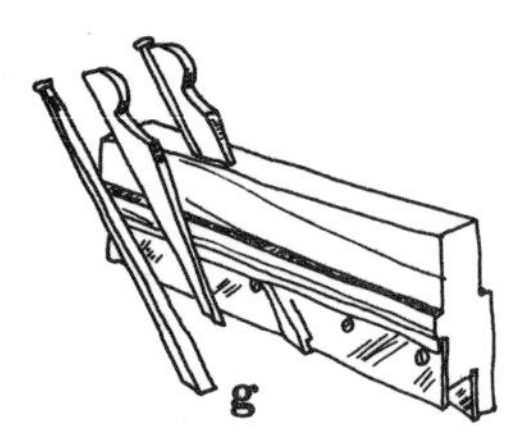

Tongue and Groove Pla

Stone Construction

Stone construction was not common in early Nova Scotia. In Halifax, the Citadel and some of the early houses and public buildings were stone, but in the rest of Nova Scotia, there was both a lack of available stone and lack of skill. Brick construction was even more uncommon, but was used for some houses in the Annapolis Valley and in Halifax. Stone construction methods have changed less than any other form of construction; thus St. Mary's Basilica in Halifax and the two churches in Sydney, St. George's and St. Patrick's, are very similar in the manner in which they were built. The stone used in Nova Scotia was of a local variety, except for granite, imported as ships' ballast. The local building stone in Halifax was

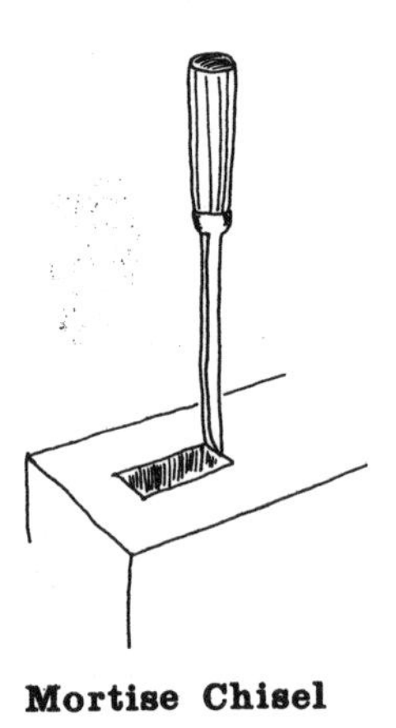

Mortise Chisel

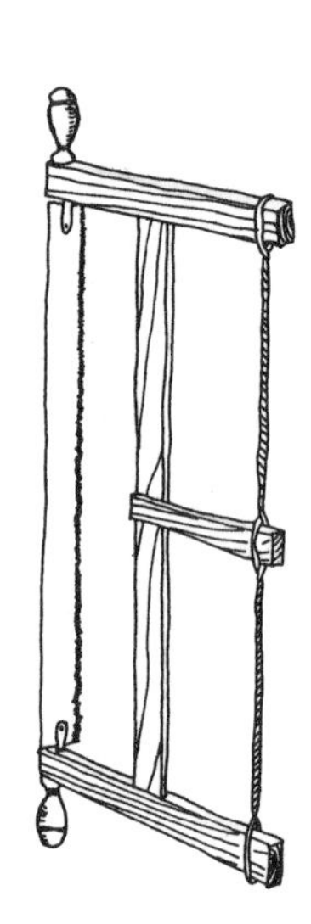

Frame Saw

ironstone, and in the Cape Breton area a variety of rubble stone was used. The practice of construction with stone, or brick, is to lay up the corners and work toward the middle of each wall using stones of roughly the same sizes. On the north wall of St. Mary's, one may see the levelling stones, the small flat stones used in the wall to bring it "up to level". Most stone on these churches is quarry dressed, or shaped and squared to approximately the same size. The trim, and window and door surrounds are of properly dressed quality. In most cases the stone used for this work is of a better grade and is often a different type of stone altogether.

The master mason would do most of the finish stonework while the journeymen would do the laying-up, but very often the carving of stone would be done by a carver who might not necessarily be a master mason. Most masons in Nova Scotia came from Scotland, and were employed by the government or the military. However, it was to be another thirty years after the building of St. Mary's Basilica, before the golden age of stone building left Halifax with a collection of richly carved and decorated stone buildings which may be seen today.

The early churches, both in stone and wood, were well constructed and have become permanent features of our cultural landscape. They remain a source of reference, and a testimony to the skill of a pioneer industry, which has evolved into the complex construction business of today. However well we build in the present and in the future, it is doubtful that the master craftsman will pass this way again. Like the wooden ships, the pegged framing and the carved altar pieces, he belongs to another age.

CHURCHES

St. Paul's, Halifax

IN HONOUR OF
IN MEMORY OF
1914 1918
1939 1945

St. Paul's, the oldest protestant church building in Canada, is indelibly linked with the founding of Halifax, for it was very much a part of the plan of settlement. When the decision was made to establish a British stronghold on the coast of Nova Scotia as a counterfoil to the fortress at Louisbourg, the British Lords of Trade and Plantations sought suitable arrangements for ministering to the colonists. In a letter dated April 6, 1749, they asked the venerable Society for the Propagation of the Gospel in Foreign Parts to appoint ministers and schoolmasters for the new settlement at Chebucto (Halifax) Harbour.

In response to this request, the Society arranged for the two clergymen and two schoolmasters to join the expedition, which was then in the final stages of preparation for the North Atlantic crossing. In a remarkably short period of 10 days, the Rev. William Tutty and the Rev. William Anwyl had been recruited, and on April 17, 1749, both were issued a license by the Bishop of London.

The Rev. William Tutty was to become the first rector of St. Paul's Church, a responsibility he assumed with great spirit and dedication. He had received a masters degree from Emmanuel College, Cambridge, and was ordained in 1748. Tutty was approximately 35 years old when he embarked for the New World. His letters bear testimony to his courage and his concern for his flock. In direct contrast, the Rev. William Anwyl, who was expected to assist Rev. Tutty failed to measure up to his responsibilities. According to Tutty "both his actions and expressions bespeak rather the boatswain of a man-o-war than a minister of the Gospel". As a consequence, Anwyl was recalled to England to answer these charges, but died, in February, 1750, before his return.

The Rev. William Tutty was probably a passenger aboard the man-o-war *Sphinx* which carried Col. Edward Cornwallis to his new appointment as Governor of Nova Scotia and Captain General of the Forces. They set sail on May 14, 1749, and arrived at Chebucto Harbour on June 21, 1749, in the van of the 13 transports which landed a total of 2576 settlers. Under the leadership of Cornwallis, they set about the arduous task of clearing and laying out the new town site. Alluding to the hardships in a letter to the Duke of Bedford, Cornwallis noted, "As there was not one yard of clear ground, Your Grace will imagine our difficulty and what work we have to do."

During the early months of settlement, divine services were conducted in the open air by Rev. William Tutty; it was not until October, when the first Government House was completed, that he was able to hold indoor services. One gathers from Mr. Tutty's writings that Government House was something less than adequate for his purpose. He spoke of the great inconvenience of conducting services in the Governor's dining room which was "not large enough to contain one fifth of those who would be glad to assemble themselves together".

The building of a church was a very important part of the overall plan of the new settlement. By July 12, 1749, the first "plan for the town" had been prepared by John Brewse, an engineer on Governor Cornwallis' staff. This original town plan, along with Charles Morris' survey plan, set aside a site for a church at the northern end of the Parade Square; the southern end was designated as a "place for the court house". However, when work began on the construction of the church, in the spring of 1750, its site had been changed to the south end. This decision was attributed to the Hon. Richard Bulkeley, the first Provincial Secretary.

From the various letters and reports written by Rev. Tutty we have a fairly complete picture of those early days of the settlement, and the significant events relating to the building of the church. For instance, in a report dated December 1, 1749, Tutty mentioned that work was underway in Boston for the production of all the framing for a church "capable of holding 900 persons". This might seem to be a very large building for such a newly settled community. But when one considers that Halifax had 6000 inhabitants within two years of its founding, half of whom were adherents of the Church of England, it can be concluded that the size of the church had been well considered. Tutty reported about construction preparations in a letter of March 17, 1750, noting: "It begins to thaw apace and as soon as the frost is quite gone, the foundation will be hard and I hope finished for the church by the time it (the frame) can arrive from Boston. It is exactly the model of Marybone Chapel".

Marybone Chapel in London, later known as St. Peter's Vere Street, was designed by James Gibbs for the Earl of Oxford. Lord Halifax, the chief Lord of Trade and Plantations, attended this London church and may have procured the architectural plans which Cornwallis brought to Nova Scotia. Certainly, the exterior detailing of St. Paul's is in the classical tradition, inspired by the work of the celebrated British architect Sir Christopher Wren, and his protégé, James Gibbs. The Palladian window, pilasters, pediments and intricate three-tier steeple all exemplify British classicism. However, the

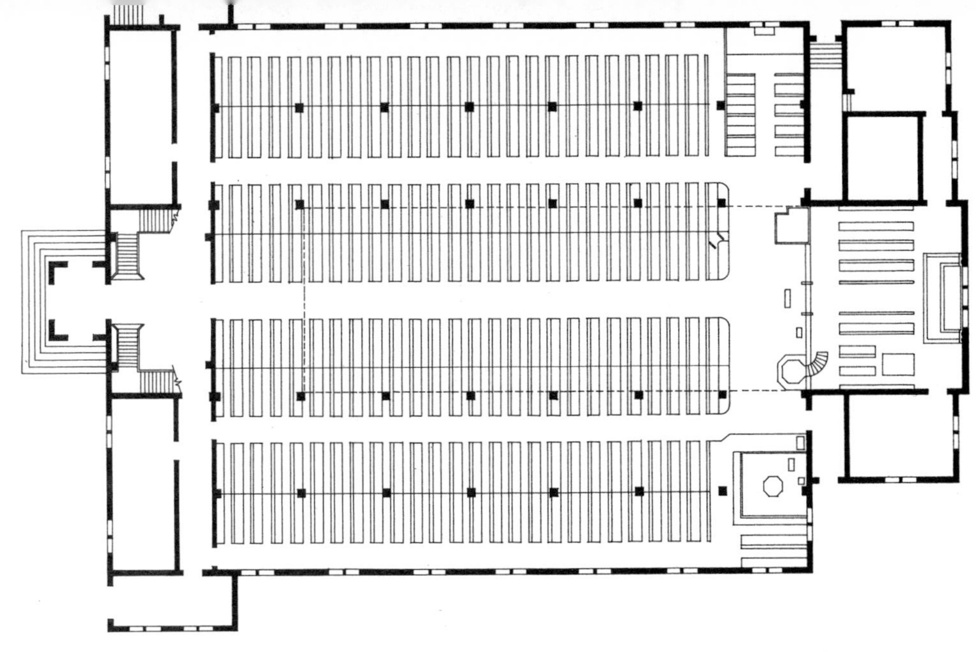

Plan

floor plan of the church, the simple rectangular auditorium with galleries on three sides of the interior, represents, distinctly, the style of a New England meeting house.

It is most probable that such items as windows, doors, glass and moulded trimming were included, along with the frame, in the shipment from Boston. Bricks were made locally, according to Cornwallis who noted, in a letter dated July 10, 1750, "30,000 bricks have been burnt here that prove very good". Most of these bricks would have been used as "brick nogging", a method of infilling the space between the main framing timbers of the exterior walls.

The cornerstone was laid on June 13, 1750, by Governor Cornwallis. The church, which was not known as St. Paul's until 1759,

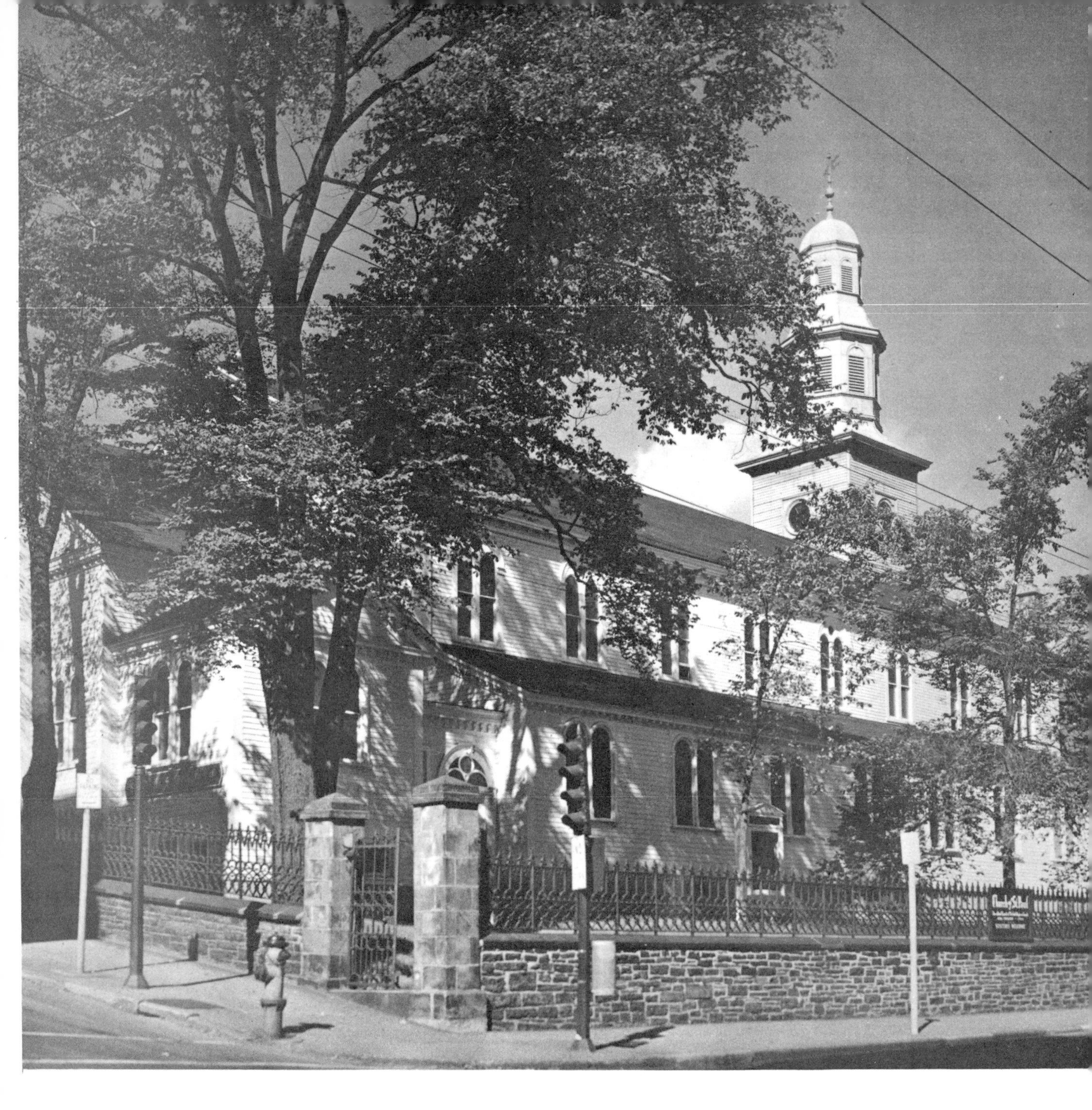

was opened for divine service on September 2, 1750. Several weeks later, Rev. Tutty duly reported, "On Sunday ye second of September I preached for the first time in the new church which when completely fitted up will be a very handsome structure." Five years passed before Rev. Breynton, Rev. Tutty's successor, could report that "the church is completely finished without and makes a handsome appearance". He also noted that the church was "aisled and plastered within and pewed after a rough fashion by the inhabitants".

In the first 40 years of the church's history, attendance in the winter months called for courage, as the building was not heated in any way. Worshippers brought with them foot warmers, consisting of iron boxes filled with burning charcoal, or wooden boxes containing heated bricks; others took their dogs to church to serve a similar purpose. In 1773, two stoves, procured from England, were presented to St. Paul's by Governor Campbell who was concerned about the prevalence of pneumonia. They were of little use for no one could be found who could prevent them from smoking. By 1788, Bishop Charles Inglis, in a letter to the wardens, voiced dislike for the chill and cold commenting, "It is indeed much to be wished that the people advanced in years, or of tender constitution could attend divine service without risk to their health, or feeling the painful sensation of cold, to both of which they are liable in the severity of winter."

Lord Campbell's stoves were put in place in 1796, but still smoked and caused great

annoyance. Finally, in 1798, two "cannon" stoves were borrowed from General Murray, the Commanding Officer of the garrison. After sufficient quantity of pipe was purchased, and chimneys built "to carry off the smoke", the two stoves were successfully installed, giving St. Paul's its first acceptable heating system at last.

In 1812, the north end of the church was extended by an additional window bay. The belfry was re-built, replicating the original, and later was sheathed in copper. The church was again enlarged in 1858, with the addition of side wings, and the windows modified by the insertion of wide, intermediate mullions. In 1872, the present chancel was added at the south end of the church.

About 1865, Mrs. W. B. Slater described the interior of St. Paul's in glowing terms, mentioning such things as the crimson curtain draping the big south window, the red velvet pulpit cushions, the old organ "with plaster and gold cherubs" and the font with "a chirpy gilt dove perched above it". In contrast, several anonymous letters appeared about the same time in the press, referring to the interior appearance of St. Paul's as "dingy and dark, small and unfitting, as the principal place of worship in a city of such importance as Halifax". One letter went as far as to suggest that the church be torn down to make way for a more impressive building of brick. Fortunately, every such suggestion was resisted, and plans were initiated for the restoration of the historic building.

Today, the interior of the church conveys a sense of quiet elegance. Natural light from the double-tiered side windows, plain on the upper level and stained glass on the lower level, enhances the lofty interior space. Fluted posts rise above the galleries to the vaulted ceiling. Stone and brass plaques line the walls, and antique, fabric hatchments, bearing the coats-of-arms of the illustrious dead, hang from the galleries. Dark stained pews and high wooden wainscotting add to the dignity of the atmosphere.

The exterior still displays the majestic symmetry and ornamentation of Georgian times. The superb Palladian window above the main entrance, the pedimented gable with rondel window, the pilasters and cornice moulding are some of the distinctive features which give the church its unique beauty. The steeple, like those of Sir Christopher Wren, is a crowning achievement; a square, saddle-back tower with rondel windows is surmounted by two octagonal lanterns each with round-headed openings and domed roofs.

Halifax has seen many changes since Col. Edward Cornwallis and the original settlers cleared the forests for their garrison town. For all these changes, however, old St. Paul's still occupies a place in the hearts of the citizens of Halifax, and a strategic site in the modern city. Situated opposite City Hall on the Grand Parade, the symbolic centre of Halifax, St. Paul's is cherished as the city's oldest landmark.

St.John's, Lunenburg

Lunenburg is distinguished by its architecture. Viewed from the harbour, the town is a stage setting of brightly coloured wooden buildings along streets that rise in gentle steps from the harbour's edge. As a long-time prosperous fishing community, the houses and shops reflect the traditions of wood construction and craftmanship; decorative woodwork, elaborate detailing, and steeply pitched roofs generate the character of Lunenburg. Nestled in the town's centre, on a well treed square, is St. John's Anglican Church, built under Royal Charter in 1753.

The settlers who founded Lunenburg were known as "foreign protestants". They were a combination of French and German speaking colonists who came to Lunenburg, in 1753, after a brief sojorn in Halifax. There were approximately 1500 settlers, and initially, their spiritual needs were administered to by Jean-Baptiste Moreau, who had been a Catholic priest in Brest, France, had then married in England and been accepted as a missionary of the Church of England after emigrating with the founders of Halifax to the New World.

Church services were held at first in open air on the site of the present church. As construction of St. John's began, building materials, including the oak frame, were shipped from Boston, for at that time, there were no nearby sawmills. There is, in fact, a belief, that the timbers for St. John's came from Old King's Chapel in Boston, which was being dismantled about the same time.

It took five years to build the church, as the community was beset with many problems, not the least of which was lack of funds. The original grant received from the Board of Trade and Plantations was insufficient to complete the church, and it took some time before additional money was approved for the building. Two sketches were made of the original church, one dated 1754, and the other 1837, each of which depicts the church as a simple, two-storey, meeting house style of building with windows at both ground and balcony levels, and a pitched roof with gable ends. Records state that the frame was "well and truly raised by the townspeople". We also learn that the rectangular plan of the church measured 58 feet by 38 feet, and that the church had a 28-foot high, flat, plastered ceiling, a balcony extending around three sides, and a large three-decker pulpit. All this may sound typical of the New England meeting house which is due to the fact that the frame did, indeed, come from Boston. There were two interesting anomalies, however, the tower at the west end and the large, round-headed window at the east end appear to be injections of two foreign elements, strangely out of place, but not without plausible explanation.

One of the unusual features in the 1754 sketch is the circular tower. Its steeply pitched, conical roof and narrow, slotted windows are reminiscent of the medieval, stone towers of the Rhineland. Quite logically, it can be assumed that this tower was the German settlers' contribution to St. John's. The other element seemingly foreign to the otherwise simple design is the large round-headed window at the east end of the building, which might be easily identified as a sampling of British classicism, a Church of England influence.

Lunenburg was not a prosperous community in the beginning, and when, in 1770, many of the Calvinists and Lutherans in the congregation established their own churches, it was feared, and even suggested, that St. John's might have to close its mission. Much to their credit, however, the somewhat depleted congregation persevered and prevailed, with the assistance of grants from the Society for the Propagation of the Gospel. The Society continued to contribute funds until 1834.

For the first fifty years the congregation worshipped in an unheated church. Unquestionably, these were difficult years, but with the appointment of Rev. T. Shreve, rector from 1804 to 1816, St. John's was revitalized. Extensive repairs to the church were carried out, and the first heating stove was probably installed during this time. Otherwise, there was no change in the outward appearance of the building until 1840, when the tower of the church was re-built. It is not clear what happened to the original circular tower; but a square gothic tower replaced the earlier tower. In any event, the new tower, measuring 12 feet by 12 feet in plan, appears to be the beginning of the gothicizing of the church. The tower was an imposing 60 feet high with corner pinnacles; the interior of the tower provided a "singing pew" for the choir in the balcony. According to the church records, W. Lawson was the builder of the 1840 tower, and the Rev. James Cochran was rector during this period. He has the distinction of being the first native-born rector.

During the ministry of Rev. Henry Owen, between 1852 and 1884, the building, once again, underwent major repairs and alterations. Between 1870 and 1875, the church was moved 25 feet to the west to make room for the addition of a chancel at the east end. The nave was extended by 10 feet and the ceiling changed from a flat ceiling to the present sloping ceiling. In addition, the present, and third, tower was built. This work was done by Sterling and Dewar, architects, and Godley and Hoppes, contractors, all of Halifax. One might wonder how moving the building was accomplished without disturbing the resting place of those early rectors and parishioners who were buried in the crypt below the church.

In 1892, the side aisles were added under the direction of Solomon Morash, a communicant of St. John's, and master craftsman in his own right. Morash was assisted by fellow parishioners who in all probability were shipwrights. Their work was the culmination of very extensive changes which completed a remarkable transformation of St. John's from the simple style of the original church to this very unusual and distinctive example of early Victorian gothic revival architecture that we see today.

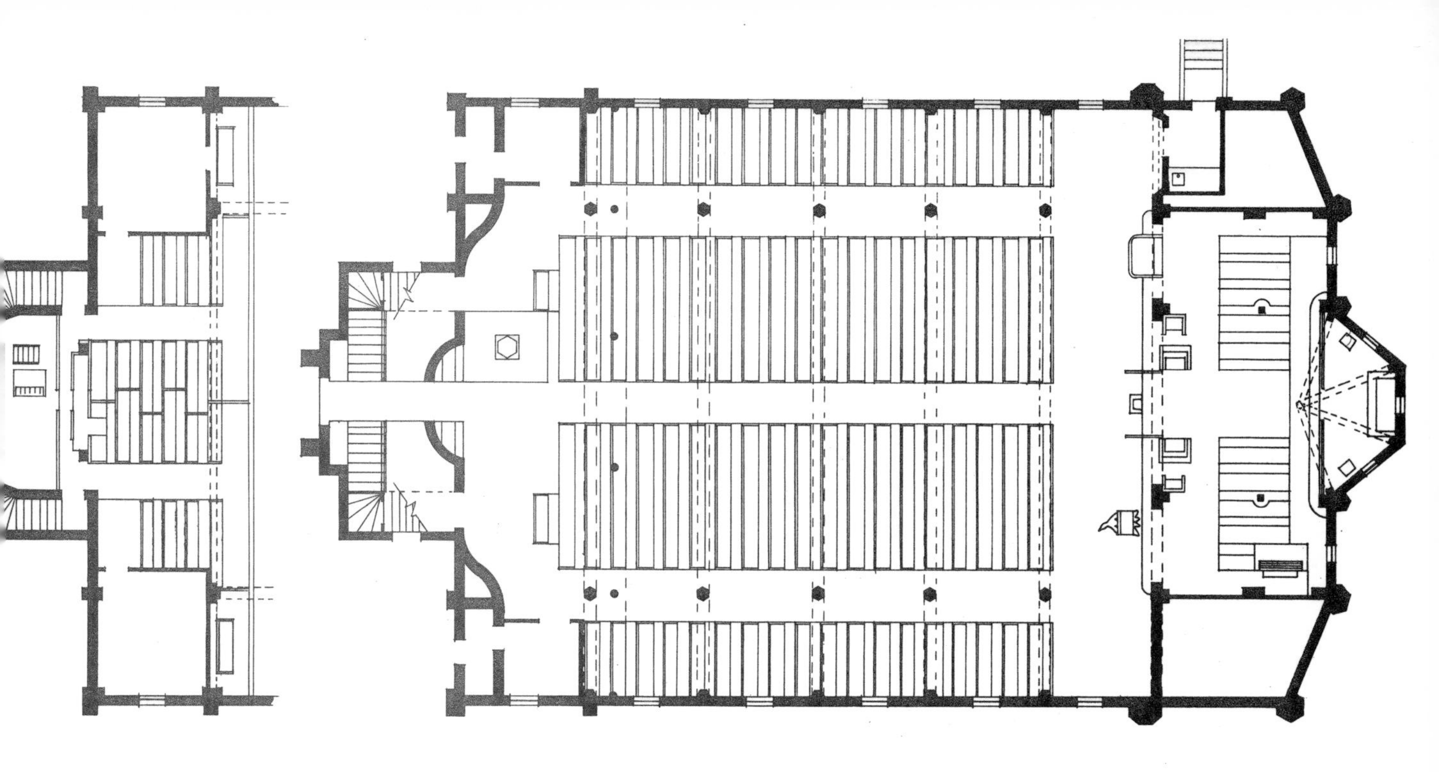

Plan

0 5 ft

The interior, too, has been gothicized in its details, and is characterized by exposed hammerbeams which form part of the roof structure. Stained dark brown, they occur at every column location and are tied together across the width of the church by steel tie rods. The roof deck is also exposed wood and finished in the same manner. The pews are finished to a dark hue and rest on the exposed wood board floor; each pew is numbered. This dark woodwork is enriched by red carpeting on the aisles. The windows are stained glass, further enhancing the interior, and plaques and memorials line the perimeter walls. The expanse of wood, and the fine fittings and furnishings, all combine to create an interior with a feeling of protective warmth.

St. John's is a striking example of a church which was "brought up to date" on numerous occasions as renovations were made. The result of so many changes is that the style of the original church building in no longer recognizable. Yet, it is an attractive example of the highly embellished, asymmetrical, gothic style, completely fashioned in wood. The church seems perfectly in keeping with the decorative houses of the town.

Lunenburg, as it has evolved from its founders, has always been known for its industrious people and their construction and shipbuilding skills. St. John's, today, is a product of this tradition, and is a landmark in this very unique town of Nova Scotia.

Little Dutch Church,
Halifax

Between 1750 and 1752, an influx of approximately 3,000 German, French and Swiss protestant settlers came to Halifax. The first ship, *Ann*, carrying 300 German settlers from the Palatinate arrived in September of 1750, and in June and July of the following year, more Germans arrived. The Swiss also began to arrive in 1751. In 1752, about 1,000 French-speaking settlers came from Montbeliard. These settlers had come to Halifax at the request of the British Board of Trade and Plantations who wanted to colonize Nova Scotia. In 1753, about 1,500, set sail for Malagash Harbour where they founded the town of Lunenburg. After the exodus, only about 25 families remained in Halifax.

The foreign protestant families settled in the "north suburb" where lots were especially laid out for them. In 1756, the settlers began construction of their own house of worship on a portion of their burial ground at the corner of Brunswick and Gerrish streets. The church records indicate that the settlers may have actually moved an existing house and reconstructed it on the site. "We had some lumber belonging to us in common, lying in our Churchyard. This lumber was exchanged with Mr. George Nagel for a house which was placed where it stands at present by voluntary hands in the year 1756". The miniature church has become known to Haligonians as the Little Dutch Church; the word "Dutch" is actually a misnomer for the word "Deutsch" or German in that language.

By 1758, the small church was properly finished inside at the expense of Otto William Schwartz whose descendants began the Schwartz spice import company which still flourishes today. It is recorded that "...walls were panelled and doors, windows, and chairs, and everything belonging to it were supplied." The condition was that Schwartz be paid without interest when they were able to do so. Today, the interior seems very austere, with plain, bench-style pews and an unadorned, barrel-vaulted, plaster ceiling. The small windows and primitive, original altar add to the pioneer atmosphere.

The original log construction measures 20 feet by 29 feet, but in 1760, it was increased in length by 11 feet. At the same time, the diminutive steeple and belfry were added. Not surprisingly, the style of the steeple is reminiscent of those found in the Vosges Mountains of Alsace not far from the Rhine. A bell was brought to Halifax for the little church from Louisbourg after the fall of the great fortress. It was purchased by a member of the congregation, Mr. George Bayer. The bell remained in the belfry until it was removed in 1842. Some years later the bell was purchased by the Château de Ramezay in "Old Montreal" where it now reposes.

On March 23, 1761, the small church was consecrated by Rev. Breynton, rector of St. Paul's, who had mastered the German language by then. The congregation, who were of Lutheran background, followed the doctrines of the Church of England, and named their church St. George's. In the early days, the schoolmaster regularly officiated reading two sermons each Sunday as well as psalms and prayers all in the German language. Once in every quarter, Rev. Breynton or Rev. Wood, his curate, would administer Holy Communion. Over the years, the close relationship with St. Paul's and the gradual anglicizing of the congregation, led to the inevitable transformation of the "German mission" into the larger congregation of St. George's Round Church, which took over the role of the little church at the beginning of the 19th century.

On the 200th anniversary of the founding of Halifax, in 1949, a memorable service was held at the Little Dutch Church. Special admittance cards were issued due to the very limited seating capacity, but the nearby streets were crowded with people, some sitting on the old stone wall, some in parked cars and some just standing on the sidewalks. Above the small, wooden door of the antique church, loud speakers broadcast the service for all to hear. Though services are only held on special occasions, the building is well cared for by its neighbouring and namesake church, St. George's Round Church.

The picturesque Little Dutch Church is often the subject of paintings, drawings or photographs. And if you wander down Brunswick Street to get your own photograph, don't be surprised if the neighbourhood children gather around and proudly acquaint you with the facts about their little church. Appreciated as a local treasure, the Little Dutch Church also has a significant place in the nation's heritage.

Meeting House, Barrington

1763

In 1761, some forty families sailed from Chatham, Eastham, and Harwich, in Cape Cod, to the southern tip of Nova Scotia where they had been granted 100,000 acres in the township of Barrington. No longer threatened by the French, after the fall of Quebec in 1759, or by the Indians, this part of Nova Scotia, with its abundant woodlands and proximity to the rich fishing grounds, attracted these people. Their settlement, at the head of Barrington Harbour, centered around the mouth of a river. Living conditions were extremely difficult, and the first winter brought many settlers near starvation. This, however, did not deter more settlers from coming; one year later, Quaker whalers from Nantucket came as well.

The first houses were log cabins, and religious services were initially held in the various homes. It is said that services were also held in a "log building further up the river", but the validity of this claim appears to be in some doubt. It was not until 1765 that work on the meeting house was started.

Joshua Nickerson, a local shipbuilder, was the "undertaker" of construction for the new meeting house. Nickerson also built Barrington's first decked vessel and first grist mill. In the construction of the meeting house, he was assisted by Elijah Swaine, a Quaker, by Magistrate Herman Kenny and by Theodore Harding. It is interesting to note that a Quaker was asked to assist in the construction of a Congregationalist meeting house, as the Congregationalists had not shown much tolerance towards Quakers at home in New England. No doubt, the rigors of settling frontier territory necessitated co-operation and lessened prejudices.

The building was large enough to accommodate 300 people. This was an ambitious project considering that the building probably would have housed the entire population of Barrington at that time. It was ambitious, too, considering that this was an entirely different type of construction; heavy timber framing, sawn lumber, and clapboard sheathing was used instead of log construction.

The meeting house measured approximately 36 feet by 30 feet and has not

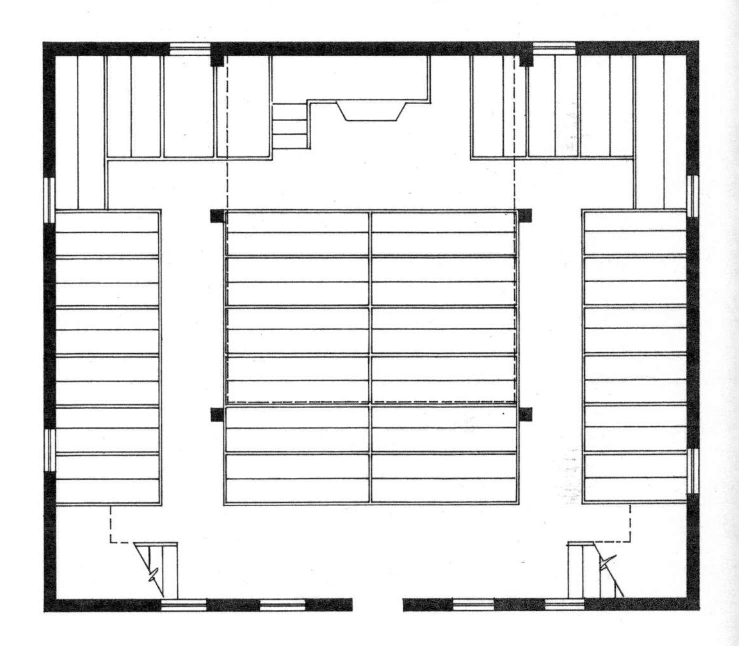

Plan

0 3 ft

been substantially altered over the years, except that shingles have replaced the original clapboard siding. It is believed that part of the oak frame came from New England and part came from wood cut on nearby Sherose Island. The two foot wide pine boards used in the construction, may have come from New England as there was no mill in Barrington to cut boards to that width.

Nickerson and his men built well, and one can see the shipbuilder's hand in the construction of "ship's knees" used to provide strength and lateral stability at the intersection of the roof and exterior walls. Axe marks are still visible in the unfinished framing members.

In November of 1767, opening services were held and people came dressed in their Cape Cod "going-to-meeting clothes". The service was conducted by Reverend Samuel Wood, the resident minister of Barrington. The congregation, however, was not wealthy and could not afford to pay a minister for his services; in exchange for his work, Wood was granted 100 acres of land at Wood's Harbour. At this time, the meeting house was incomplete being without windows, door, seats, and stove. As a result, in severe weather and during wintertime, services were held in the homes of local residents. In summer, the services in the meeting house probably followed the traditional pattern of an "exercise" in the forenoon and one in the afternoon.

Samuel Wood left Barrington in 1771. Four years later, he joined the Continental Army, and was later taken prisoner, and died. Following Wood's departure, two young Cape Cod preachers served at Barrington intermittently, but the meeting house was neglected during this period when the strains of the American Revolution were felt by the former Americans now living in Nova Scotia. Even as late as 1786, the building still had no door or windows. It is believed that the door, windows, and pulpit, were finally installed in the 1780's or 1790's.

Later, in 1814, a Board of Trustees was appointed to oversee the building, and shares were sold for two pounds to raise money for repairs. The meeting house was opened "for all preachers of the gospel" no matter what denomination. However, not all of the plans were realized, and the building remained in a state of disrepair. As with its New England counterparts, the meeting house was used for secular purposes as well as for worship, but eventually, the use of the building for town meetings was discontinued. This change occurred in November, 1838, according to the minutes of the meeting which stated, "the town meeting was held on the earth by the side of the old meeting house (the doors of which have been shut against the town)".

In 1841, box pews and a plaster ceiling were installed by the Presbyterians and Baptists, and by this time a stove was also installed. By 1850, however, due to the building of other churches in the vicinity, the meeting house stood unused and deserted. In 1890, a decision was made to demolish the building. A provincial act was passed two

years later authorizing its removal. Miraculously, because of an official's illness, these instructions were not carried out, and the building survived.

The Anglicans used the meeting house for the period between 1916 and 1934, after which the building was taken over by the Cape Sable Historical Society and maintained as a tourist attraction.

The architectural style of the meeting house is New England vernacular. It is symmetrical, barn-like in form, and finished by a steeply pitched roof. It is natural that the early settlers would have brought with them the legacy of the meeting house design. Indeed, this association was reinforced as some of the material for the building was cut and shipped from New England. The wooden building is typical of the style of meeting house prevalent in the 1700's in New England. It has a rectangular plan with the pulpit on one long side and the door opposite. A gallery runs around three sides of the interior. In keeping with the Puritan ethic, ornamentation, both inside and outside, is practically non-existent except for some moulding detail at the exterior corners and two curious diamond-shaped frames at each gable end. Tradition has it that the residents of the community, at one time, knew it was mid-day when the sun struck the face of the diamond at the western gable. On the diamond at the eastern gable, there is the painted face of a clock, which may have once been part of a sun dial.

Although the interior of the building is

plain, there is an elaborately constructed and fitted pulpit. In the evolution of the meeting house, the pulpit, box pews, and doors were built when embellishment was eventually being accepted.

The meeting house stands on a grassy knoll on a sharp curve of the highway. Beside the meeting house is a cemetery where the earliest stones date back to 1766. By constructing the meeting house, the builders demonstrated commitment to their new homeland, and their building is as sound today as when it was first built — a remarkable achievement considering the extreme age of the building and the long periods of neglect that it endured.

The Barrington Meeting House is the last of five Congregationalist meeting houses built in Nova Scotia prior to 1770 by the early New England settlers. Saved by fate from destruction, it remains as Canada's oldest non-conforming house of worship.

St. George's, Sydney

St. George's Anglican Church dates from the founding of Sydney, in 1785, when a townsite was cleared and laid out by new settlers and the men of the 33rd British Regiment under the direction of Major J.F.W. DesBarres. Desbarres was a renowned military engineer who had won distinction in the capture of the French fortress at Louisbourg in 1758, and who had surveyed and charted the coast of Nova Scotia from 1765 to 1773. He became not only the founder of Sydney but the first Lieutenant-Governor of the colony of Cape Breton which remained independent from the rest of Nova Scotia until 1820.

During 1785 and 1786, streets were laid out and sites were chosen for barracks, administration buildings, and for St. George's Church. Following the first official parish meeting of the new church on September 27, 1785, work commenced on the church building.

Since the 33rd Regiment had participated in the demolition of Louisbourg, it may be reasonable to assume that much of the stone used for the church came from the dismantled fortress. Indeed, it is said that the quoin stones at the corners of the building and the jamb stones around the doors and windows are a type of coarse sandstone known to have been quarried in Caen, France, and shipped to Louisbourg in the holds of ships.

St. George's was built to serve as the garrison chapel as well as a parish church. For this reason, the British Parliament financed the initial construction with £500 and later, in 1803, added a grant of £300. St. George's remained the garrison church until 1854 when the resident garrison was withdrawn for service in the Crimean War.

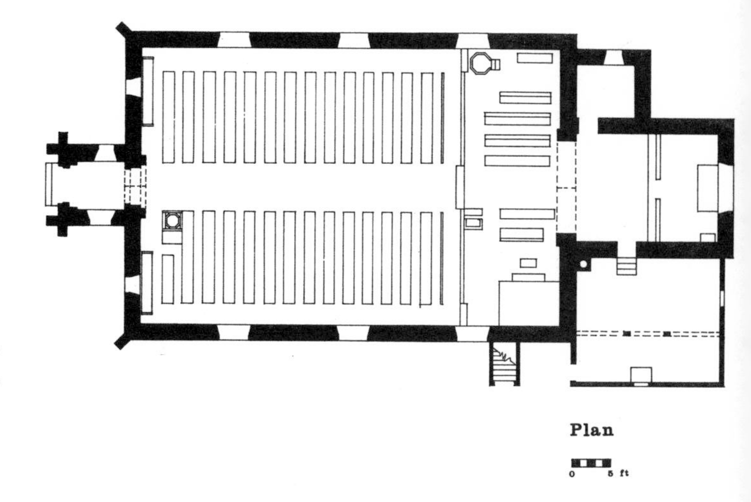

Plan

Construction proceeded and, by 1790, the exterior was completed, the floors laid, and the first services held. This original building was later described by the Rev. R. J. Uniacke as having, "...consisted simply of a nave, a plain building, constructed of grey stone, about sixty feet long, having three large circular headed windows upon each side, with a large venetian window at the east end".

In 1821, a wooden tower with cupola was placed in a central position on the roof. The weight of the tower, however, soon weakened a side wall and, in 1839, the tower was removed. A new wooden tower and steeple, 96 feet high, was then constructed at the western end of the old stone church. The new steeple and repairs were financed by the Imperial government, which had made money available from the Coal Mine Reserve Fund.

In spite of these repairs, however, the structure had seriously deteriorated by 1858. The following year, work was started on a major reconstruction program. Rev. Uniacke, then rector, described the condition of the church, recording that "upon the old roof being removed, the wall, which had been leaning to an alarming degree, collapsed of its own weight". He went on to say that the church was "rebuilt from its old foundation in 1859, in the gothic style, with open roof and pointed windows, slightly ornamented with stained glass".

In 1863, a chancel and vestry were added, both built of stone. Ten years later, another catastrophe befell St. George's. On August 24, 1873, gale force winds toppled the steeple tower. For days the steeple lay on the ground across Charlotte Street. It was not until 1875, that a special meeting of the congregation was called to consider the rebuilding of the tower. It was decided to proceed, but this time the tower was to be built in stone framed in heavy timber and clad with metal.

The strong stone steeple was crowned with a device which afforded some amusement. Dr. W. McLeod referred to the device in his memoirs as having been "fearfully and wonderfully made, and possibly having some mysterious significance not to be understood by ordinary mortals". In 1888, Bishop Courtney visited Sydney and congratulated the parishioners of St. George's on the fine new spire; then, he quipped, "As for that thing on top of the spire, I hereby give you my episcopal authority to fall down and worship it if you wish; you break no law, for it is like nothing that is in the heavens above, nor in the earth beneath, nor in the waters under the earth". No description of the "thing" remains, but it was soon replaced with a plain cross.

One last trial occurred on August 27, 1888, when lightning struck the steeple. The damage was repaired and the steeple has remained sound in the ensuing years.

"St. George's Church, by a continuous and unbroken chain, connects, as perhaps no other institution connects, the new Sydney of today with the primitive Sydney of the Eighteenth Century." So wrote the Venerable Archdeacon Smith in commemorating the first seventy years of the parish. His words remain all the more true in this 20th century. St. George's Church, surprisingly small in scale, its stones darkened with age, conjures up memories of the rough-hewn town and sturdy settlers of long ago.

Old Holy Trinity, Middleton

On the outskirts of the town of Middleton, Old Holy Trinity Anglican Church may be found amid its tombstones in a peaceful wooded grove. In the mid-18th century this area, with its air of quiet antiquity, marked the centre of a parish which embraced about 500 square miles of the Annapolis Valley. At that time, the area was known as Wilmot.

In 1782, Rev. John Wiswall was sent out as a missionary to the districts of Cornwallis, Horton, and Wilmot. He was, like many of the people he ministered to, a United Empire Loyalist from New England. He, himself, was a native of Boston, Massachusetts, and had formerly been a Congregationalist pastor. He was later converted to the Episcopal church, and when anti-Loyalist terrorism forced him to leave the United States, he went first to Oxford, England, where he served as a curate until his appointment to the wilds of Nova Scotia.

In 1788, Rev. Wiswall's immense territory was divided into two parishes and a year later, he became the first rector of the newly-created parish of Wilmot. With a grant of £200 from Governor John Parr, work began, in the fall of 1789, on the new church building which would replace the log cabin that had previously served as schoolhouse and chapel. Construction of the new church progressed slowly due to the hardships of pioneer life. As Rev. Wiswall noted in a report to the Society for the Propagation of the Gospel, his flock were "in general very poor, having none of the conveniences and few of the necessities of life".

Nevertheless, by 1791, the structure was ready to the point that the congregation could assemble there for the first service, which took place on August 14. As well, the church was consecrated in that year. And by 1792, the church was finished except for "plastering, pewing and underpinning". Still later, in 1797, one of the Wardens and two Vestrymen were charged with the duties of obtaining materials for completing the interior, erecting a steeple, and installing the bell which had been donated back in 1792.

While these three churchmen must have contributed considerable time in seeing to the finishing touches of the church, Rev. Wiswall, himself, did much of the actual building with his own hands. In fact, he became so wrapped up in his labours for the congregation of Old Holy Trinity, that he was rebuked by Bishop Charles Inglis for neglecting other parts of his mission. When Wiswall repeatedly failed to fulfill his preaching duties at Aylesford (Auburn), the Bishop wrote, on August 14, 1796, saying: "Surely there must be some good reason for this. A single sermon and service in eight weeks can be of little avail either to edify or awaken people from the miserable lukewarmness and neglect about religion which so generally prevail."

One can sympathize, however, with Rev. Wiswall for his devotion to the people of Wilmot. He was undoubtedly experiencing the time-consuming pleasure not only of establishing a congregation, but also of creating a beautiful and civilized piece of

architecture in a sparsely populated wilderness. The building of Holy Trinity was probably the culmination of his long years of service as a pioneer spiritual leader, for when the church was finally completed in 1797, Wiswall was well into his sixties. It is fitting that, in 1812, at the age of 81 years, Wiswall was laid to eternal rest beside his beloved church.

Rev. Wiswall is now commemorated as "the first clergyman of any denomination who settled in this place", and his church is the treasured legacy of his contribution to that early Nova Scotia society. Fortunately, over the years the church has been maintained as much as possible in its original condition.

The exterior is of white-painted clapboard with three large, many-paned, rectangular windows on each side. Smaller gothic windows add symmetry to the entrance façade of the church, while an oversize, round-headed window is found on the chancel end. Simple mouldings appropriately decorate each of the window styles.

The steeple is a very attractive feature consisting of a large square tower surmounted by a contrasting narrow octagonal belfry and slim rounded spire. The belfry and spire are flanked by four peaked finials linked together by a delicate railing. In the base of the tower, an immense front door measures four feet wide and has huge, hand-made hinges and latch of wrought iron. The door has square-cut detailing, a Georgian pediment above, and pilasters on either side.

On entering the nave, one is immediately struck by an impression of spaciousness and light. The enormous windows, all with clear glass, admit so much daylight that there is no need for artificial light. And indeed, there are no light fixtures of any kind. The centre aisle is very wide, displaying the old pine floorboards, about 24 inches in width, with hand-forged, square-headed nails. On either side of the aisle, row on row, are the long, rectangular, box-style pews which are painted light grey. The perimeter of the pews is highlighted with brown-painted, moulded trim. The pew doors are decorated with square moulding and hand-wrought black, iron hinges. The pew doors and hinges are so eye-catching that some have been carried off by tourists. Now, replicas are in place and only the well-trained eye can tell the difference.

At the front of the nave, to the right, is the

original round pulpit on a high pedestal with steps leading up to it at one side. And along the walls, at intervals, are decorative pilasters which have been "marbleized" by an ingenious technique. Grey paint was applied and while it was still wet, it was stroked with a feather that had been dipped in coal tar, thus creating a "marble" effect.

In the stairwell leading to the gallery there is an example of a primitive solution to pioneer builder's problem. Often, in the early stages of glass technology, glass was of different thicknesses and difficult to cut exactly rectangular. Here, one of the window panes consists of two pieces of overlapping glass.

The gallery, itself, is very large and empty except for a couple of movable, bench-style pews that remain. The railing across the front of the gallery is very attractive with a row of delicately turned slim posts. Behind the gallery in the large open "bell-room", one can gaze up through the inside of the slim belfry and spire. A central "mast" with a whorl of struts has been added to brace the spire. Some early construction methods may also be observed in the "bell-room"; where a piece of plaster has come away, the original split birch laths are visible and in other cases, there are original boards cut with an upright saw. If one follows the trap door, high in the wall, which leads to the area between the ceiling and the roof, a further construction technique can be seen; birch bark was used in the roof between the decking and the shingles just as tar paper would be used today.

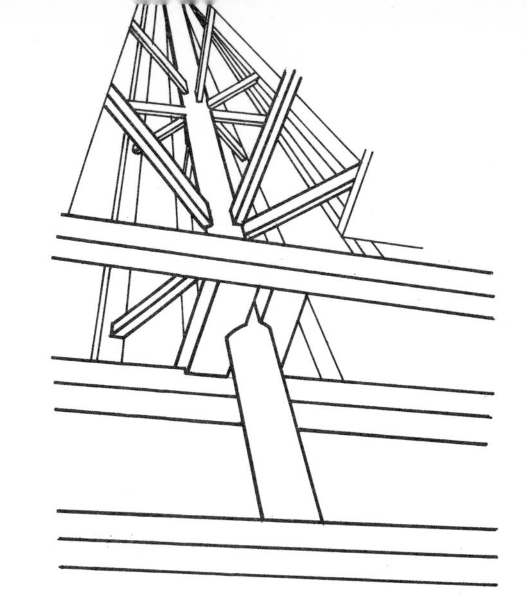

Tower Framing

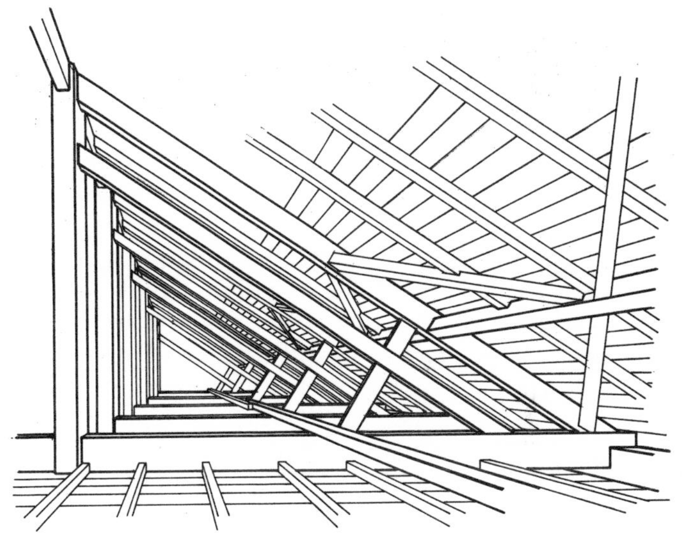

Roof Framing

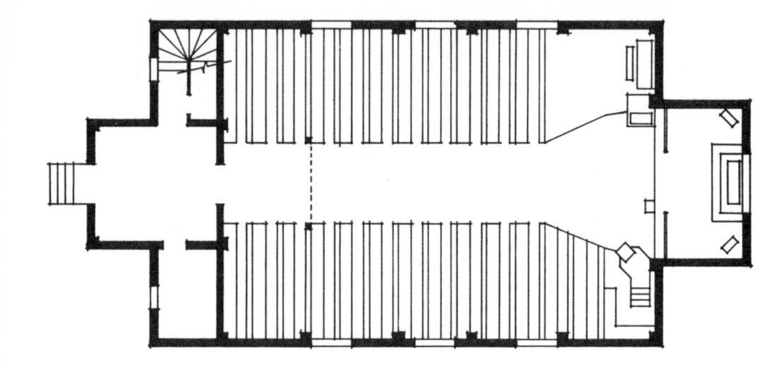

Plan

The antique bell is no longer in the belfry, but it is still being used by the present-day congregation in the belfry of the "new" Holy Trinity Church. The newer and much smaller church was built closer to the centre of the town in 1893. Thus, for almost a century, Old Holy Trinity has not been used for regular Sunday services. It is, however, used for special events such as weddings and baptisms; as well, an annual service is held there on the third Sunday in June. And from May to September, the Church is open each day for visitors, with guides available for information.

In 1950, a severe storm caused considerable damage to Old Holy Trinity. The decision whether to restore or tear down the aged structure had to be made. Fortunately, the course of restoration was chosen for the church "because of its historic value, its hallowed memories, and its own unique beauty". No better decision could have been made.

West Front

St. Mary's, Auburn

Of all the lovely old rural churches still to be found in Nova Scotia, St. Mary's Anglican Church at Auburn certainly is one of the most outstanding architecturally. In the words of the Rev. Kennedy B. Wainwright, a former rector: "St. Mary's is a near perfect adaptation in wood of the more monumental stone architecture of English designers of a slightly earlier period. Instead of reproducing stone detail in wood, the builder of St. Mary's, in the same fashion as his New England counterparts, chose to reduce classical pediments, capitals and other architectural detail to a scale suited to his materials. The result is a delicacy of scale of great charm which gives to the interior a serene and quiet intimacy."

The Auburn area was mainly settled by United Empire Loyalists in 1784. Nova Scotia's first Bishop, Charles Inglis, who was a fiery Loyalist himself, preferred the sylvan setting of Auburn in the Annapolis Valley to the fogs and drafts of Halifax. He resided at "Clermont", his Auburn estate, for 21 of the 29 years of his episcopacy. Even today, there are reminders that St. Mary's was the beloved parish church of Bishop Inglis. Just as he described on October 10, 1790, shortly after he had consecrated the church, "A pew is set apart for the Governor, and another for the Bishop in perpetuity....The King's Arms are placed over the former and the Arms of the See over the latter." The two special pews face each other near the chancel; the antique Coats of Arms, said to have been hand-painted by the Bishop himself, still designate the occupants.

Colonel James Morden, who had fought with Wolfe at Quebec, gave six acres of land for the building of St. Mary's. Morden was not a Loyalist but an Englishman who worked as Ordinance Keeper in Halifax, and who had a 5000 acre land grant in the Annapolis Valley. Col. Morden also made a substantial contribution of approximately £165 to the construction expenses, along with Governor John Parr who gave approximately £222.

Information about the builders, along with a good deal of fascinating detail about the actual construction of the church, was documented and carefully sealed in one of the copper balls, atop the beautiful steeple of St. Mary's. Having been placed there in 1790, these documents were not to be seen again for a hundred years. Then in 1890, the weather vane was blown to the ground in a heavy gale and the topmost copper ball cracked open to reveal the papers.

St. Mary's was built by William Matthews, a Master Builder, with the assistance of three local workmen: Jabex Benedict, a brick maker, his brother Michael, a stone mason, and Benjamin Foster, who split pine chunks for the roof shingles. Matthews, himself, was not from the area. He may have been employed at either the Dockyard or Ordinance Yard in Halifax, and may have been commissioned to build the church by Col. Morden. Matthews was responsible for overseeing the construction and preparing the plans; probably, he did most of the skilled work such as the intricate, classical mouldings

around the windows and central doorway.

Not only is it interesting to learn about those who were responsible for building St. Mary's, but equally interesting to have an insight into the process of building a church in the late 18th century. As might be expected, there was a good stand of pine trees in the vicinity which probably provided all the timbers necessary for framing, boarding, shingling and finishing. A sawpit was also conveniently located nearby where the rough and finished boarding, including the exterior clapboards, were whip-sawed. The hand-hewn timber frame was assembled on the ground and then raised into position with iron-pointed "pike poles". All the frames for the doors and windows were brought from Halifax by horses. Also, all the nails used in the church were hand-forged at Halifax, made up in 10 to 15 pound packages and transported by a company of soldiers who walked the distance (approximately 100 miles) by way of the old military road. It is also recorded that lime for plaster was brought from St. John, New Brunswick, and when a shortage occurred, quahog shells, which had been left by the Acadians on the beach at French Cross (Morden), were brought to Auburn and burned to make up the deficit.

William Matthews' church, fashioned in those pioneer ways, is a masterpiece of civilized classical elegance. Dignified corner pilasters with Doric capitals embellish both the main structure and the tower. The round-headed windows, set in finely moulded keystone arches, grace the north, south and west façades. A superb palladian window decorated the chancel outside and inside. The main entrance, flanked by double side pilasters, has a moulded keystone arch over the doorway surmounted by a classical pediment. The cornices were deeply moulded, and the returns were extended on the west and east gables to create the illusion of a pediment.

The steeple, a veritable work of art, was probably inspired by Col. Morden who had seen, and no doubt remembered, the great spires of the celebrated English architect, Sir Christopher Wren. The square tower has four rondel windows with keystones, and a roof with an attractive belcast flair. The roof is surmounted by an octagonal lantern ringed with keystone arches, and finished with an octagonal cap, slender spire, finial, and pennant-shaped weathervane.

The interior is a blend of pioneer styles and sophisticated classical details. High wainscotting made of very wide boards laid horizontally contrasts with the fluted pillars beneath the west gallery, and the detailed romanesque arch of the chancel opening. The latch and bolt on the main door add a primitive note while the decorative mouldings around the windows and on the pews add a civilized touch.

When St. Mary's was completed, at a total cost of £475, Bishop Charles Inglis noted that "it is the neatest, best finished church in the province". And St. Mary's has undergone very few alterations during its 192 year history. In 1826, the two side galleries, supported by slender pillars with classical capitals, were constructed. In 1865, the doors were removed from the original pews to allow the heat from the newly-installed stove to circulate to those chilly pioneer feet. In 1890, the chancel, originally only eight feet deep, was cut from the nave and moved eastward about 15 feet. On the south side of the new chancel, an alcove was built on to accommodate the organ; on the north side, a vestry was added.

Recently, St. Mary's was fortunate enough to escape total destruction. At 2 a.m. on September 20, 1981, St. Mary's beautiful steeple was struck by lightning during an electrical storm. A neighbour and a passerby both called for help, and four volunteer fire departments, from Aylesford, Berwick, Kingston, and Kentville, responded quickly to the calls. When Father Langley MacLean arrived at the scene at 3 a.m., he found a group of parishioners anxiously awaiting the outcome. Meanwhile, the firemen were having some difficulty; the water pressure in the hoses was not strong enough to reach the flames at the top of the spire. Father MacLean suggested that the parishioners should pray for the safety of their beloved, old church. And as they prayed, some standing and some on bended knee, a strong gust of wind came and forced the water from the firemen's hoses onto the flames. This fact was verified by firemen when they came down from the ladders; they had felt that a greater Power had helped them with their task.

Thus, by the quick efforts of the volunteer firefighters with the help of a small miracle, St. Mary's was rescued from ruin. The top of the beautiful steeple, which was damaged, has been completely restored to its original beauty. Thankfully, St. Mary's can still be enjoyed as the great historic and architectural treasure that it is.

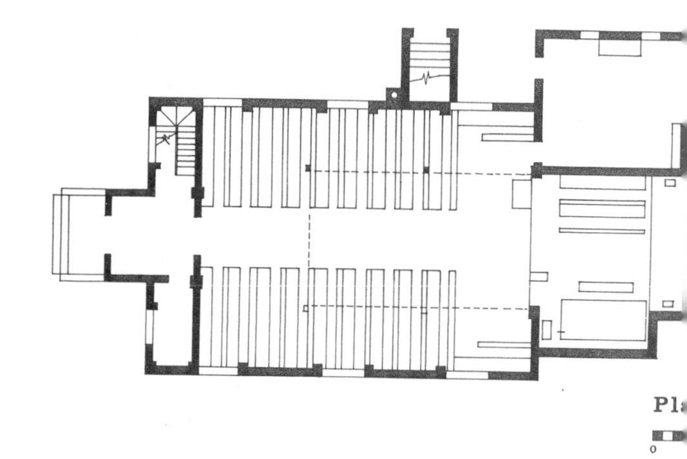

Christ Church, Karsdale

In 1605, an expedition of French explorers, led by Sieur de Monts and Samuel de Champlain, founded the Habitation at Port Royal on the sheltered shores of the Annapolis Basin. While this settlement lasted only eight years, other early settlers came to the area, including the Scots who set up a colony at Port Royal in 1629, and the New Englanders who, more than a century later in 1760, began to colonize this township of Granville. The United Empire Loyalists started arriving from the Thirteen Colonies in 1782.

Today, it is not hard to imagine the past in this antique area of Canadian civilization. The French Habitation has been reconstructed on its original site at Port Royal and, just a few miles down the secluded country road, one can find the genuine, old Anglican church at Karsdale.

The village of Karsdale, first known as Lower Granville and renamed in honour of the British victory at Kars in the Crimean War, is not more than a scattering of houses. Christ Church is set back from the roadside amid tall trees and old gravestones; the sloping land of the churchyard leads upwards to North Mountain behind the church, and provides a beautiful view downwards over the basin.

Built in 1791, according to the wishes of Bishop Charles Inglis, Nova Scotia's first Bishop, Christ Church is a plain structure with long, slim gothic windows and clapboard cladding. There is little exterior detail except for the simple but decorative mouldings that outline the tops of the window-arches. The square steeple, with unadorned rectangular belfry openings and a pointed, belcast roof, adds to the air of sturdy simplicity of this pioneer church.

In September of 1789, Bishop Inglis had visited the district and advised the inhabitants to build a church. He had also specified that the building should be 46 feet long by 30 feet wide. The main body or nave of the church, exclusive of the steeple and chancel, fits the Bishop's specifications. This suggests that the steeple and chancel were not part of the original structure but added later. While this may be true, the austere design of the steeple and its complete lack of ostentatious detail indicate that if it was added after 1791, then it was certainly not many years afterward. For about the same time, much loftier and fancier spires were being achieved in neighbouring parishes; undoubtedly, the parishioners of Christ Church would have followed the vogue unless, as is probably the case, their steeple was already completed. Certainly, Bishop Inglis, himself, gave some proof as to the date of completion of Christ Church. In 1791, he visited the church and noted that it had been "raised". And on July 12, 1793, Bishop Inglis certified that the building was completed "according to contract", and that the last payment should be made to the builders.

The interior of Christ Church, though not unchanged since its Loyalist days, still retains much of its pioneer charm. High wainscotting of very wide, plain boards, now painted grey, runs along the walls. The long windows have clear, antique glass and louvered interior shutters to fit their gothic shape. The once high, old-fashioned, rounded pulpit is still in use though its pedestal has been shortened.

In the summer of 1912, the nave was refurbished with new hardwood floors and open, bench-style pews. However, if one follows the narrow, sharply-turning staircase to the gallery, one may see the original, wide pine floorboards and a few straight-backed pews enclosed by doors. The gallery, no longer in use, has been closed in and houses a furnace which replaced the two stoves which formerly heated the church. The Loyalists would, of course, have braved bitter temperatures without any such heating devices unless they brought their own foot-warmers!

In the mid-1950's, a round-headed stained glass window was installed in the chancel replacing the old, gothic-style window. The stained glass window, which cost $2,000, commemorates the bishops of Nova Scotia; it depicts the figure of Christ wearing a crown and holding a lantern. There is some evidence, too, that the chancel was, at some time, extended, as there is a visible ridge in the plaster and some irregularities in the wainscotting. The wainscotting in the chancel, unlike that of the nave, has square-moulded detailing which likely means that the chancel was added to the original body of the church. However, the small size and simplicity of the chancel indicate that it, like the steeple, must have been an early addition.

Just as the village of Karsdale underwent a change of name, so did Christ Church. On September 1, 1793, Bishop Inglis had consecrated the church as St. Paul's Church. Nearly one hundred years later, in 1882, the church officially assumed the name of Christ Church, a name which had belonged to an earlier church in Upper Granville which had since fallen into disuse and been demolished.

Thus, the church at Karsdale has been known throughout its second century as Christ Church. Services are still held once a month in the historic church. And on Easter Sunday, the combined congregations of Annapolis Royal, Karsdale, and Granville Centre, come to Christ Church to celebrate an ancient Christian tradition just as the early settlers did so many years before.

Old St. Edward's, Clementsport

Old St. Edward's, at Clementsport, is one of the oldest and certainly one of the most interesting of the early churches of Nova Scotia. It is an outstanding example of the New England meeting house prototype, clearly displaying its pioneer origin, in general proportion and method of construction, while at the same time, harmonizing with the overtones of classical detail. It is this melding of a basic architectural form with an adaptation of pure classical detail that makes St. Edward's one of the real treasures among the early churches of Nova Scotia.

In May of 1790, Bishop Charles Inglis wrote to the Society for the Propagation of the Gospel that, "the inhabitants of Clements, amounting to 50 families, and mostly Loyalists, have petitioned the Government for money to build a church". Interestingly enough, this group of Loyalists were of English and Dutch descent with names like Jones, Shaw and Purdy, or Boehme, Vroom and Van Horn. And so it came about that St. Edward's was built on a high wooded hill overlooking the Annapolis Basin. The land was purchased for "one pepper corn" from one Dowe Ditmars according to a deed dated February 26, 1797; a later deed indicates he finally accepted 5 shillings. The site was described by Bishop Inglis as "an elevated spot on Mr. Ditmars' land and near the very center of the settlement". And, being a wooded site, the timber used in the building came from the cleared land.

It was not until 1841 that St. Edward's obtained its own rector. For the first half century, the rectors of Digby and Annapolis preached alternately at St. Edward's. Also, in the early years, services were opened with a hymn sung in Dutch, in deference to those parishioners from Holland. Today, several Dutch prayer books remain at St. Edward's.

Like many of the early church buildings, the foundations and interior piers are of fieldstone laid in random rubble. They support a typical heavy post and beam frame of hand-hewn timbers, connected by mortise and tenon joints and fastened with wooden pegs. The heavy timber members of the roof trusses are similarly fastened. If most of the timber was shaped or sawn from trees felled on Ditmars' land, it is apparent that they found a beautiful stand of primeval pine trees with sufficient girth to provide clapboards for the side walls, long hand-shaved shingles for the roof and floorboards up to 26 inches in width.

Perhaps the outstanding features of St. Edward's are the two exterior doors: one single door on the west front and the double doors on the south side. Both entrances are nicely detailed. The west entrance with its shouldered architrave and finely moulded pediment above, sets off an unusually wide door with six raised panels. The south entrance, said to have been reserved for bridal parties, and for bringing in the coffin at a funeral, is also interesting in its detail. There is an arched opening with a moulded architrave around the arch which is finished with a typical keystone.

An extra dimension to this unusual entrance is provided by the narrow pilaster-like panels on either side which are capped with simple brackets and a nicely detailed pediment.

In all, there are eleven large round-headed windows, a small rondel window in the west gable end, and a lovely Palladian window in the chancel end. The windows are simply detailed with architraves and keystones, and have a double-hung sash. It is probable that, originally, all the round-headed windows would have had the same type of fan-lighted window head as does the Palladian window in the chancel.

The charm of St. Edward's can probably be attributed to several of its unique characteristics, but part of that charm is the small steeple rising out of a square tower set slightly back from the west end. The tower or belfry has four round-headed louvred windows, and if one is willing to climb the staircase within, a beautiful countryside is there for the viewing. For more than 30 years after the church was built, an oil lamp was hoisted up into the belfry to guide ships through the Digby Gut. The truncated steeple above the tower is topped with a weathervane. The church is rectangular in plan, measuring 52 feet by 34 feet, with a very small chancel at its east end. The building is actually set on a true east-west axis, for when the shadow of the cornice touches the round window in the west façade, it is 12 o'clock noon. It is said that this was calculated to be a convenient community timepiece. The building was originally clad with clapboard, but over the years much of the original cladding has been replaced. However, it appears that the clapboard on the east end is original.

The interior of the church is quite plain and simple with a balcony at the west end and the chancel at the east end. The walls and ceiling are plastered, the plaster having been made with lime obtained by burning clam shells on the beach. The ceiling itself has the appearance of an arched vault with a flattened centre. A block of box pews with handmade hinges extends nearly to the chancel steps in the center of the church. In the forward part of this block stood the pulpit with a sounding board overhead. The pulpit was removed to its present position at the south side of the chancel in 1848, but the sounding board remains to this day in its original location. At the back of the church, to the left of the main entrance, there was, at one time, a hole in the floor where a large ring had been placed to chain the slaves during church service. When the day arrived that they were no longer slaves, four pews were installed to accommodate them. The balcony itself is supported by 14 inch ocatagonal columns which are joined at the ceiling by a distinctive wooden arch.

It is inevitable that in the long life of a church congregation there will be bad times as well as good times, and it seems that Old St. Edward's had fallen upon bad times in the years just prior to 1890. The "Golden Age" of Nova Scotia had come to an end during the 1870's and a degree of prosperity did not appear again until the 1890's. This could well explain why St. Edward's suffered such neglect and decay that, in March 1891, the congregation sought the permission of the Bishop "to use certain parts of the old church to construct a new building". It is difficult to imagine that such a thought could cross the mind of anyone familiar with the history and architectural charm of Old St. Edward's. Fortunately, good sense and reason prevailed for when permission was granted to build a new church, no authorization was given to strip and destroy the old church.

It can be assumed that the new church, which was larger and more conveniently

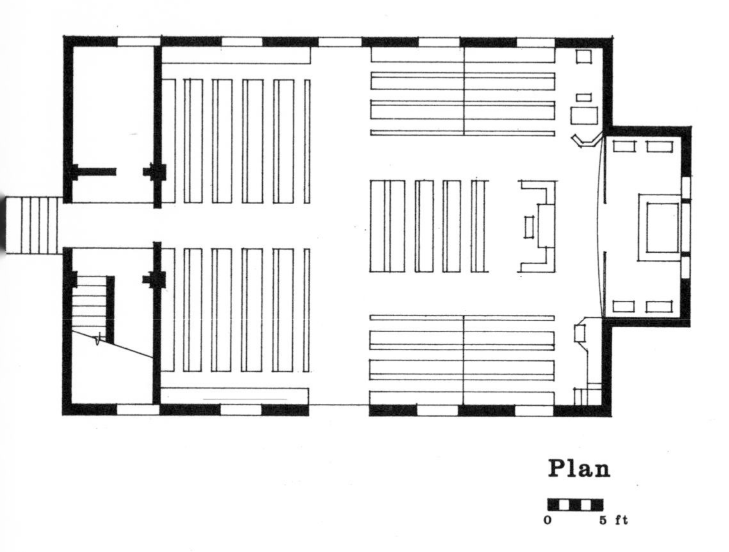

Plan

located, met the needs of the congregation, but it is interesting to note that the congregation still recognized the architectural and historical merits of their old church building. They did not share the view of their rector who was on the point of having the building demolished. Had his view prevailed a stone monument and plaque in the middle of the old cemetery would have been the only reminder of where St. Edward's once stood. It was a latent sentimental regard for the old church that saved it from an ignominious end. We learn this by reading the reminiscences of L.V. Shaw, a parishioner who told of returning from the United States in 1911, to find the church and grounds "in a deplorable state of neglect and decay". His deep concern was shared by enough church members, both at home and abroad, that they set about securing sufficient funds to clear up the old church yard and build a retaining wall along the old road. This was the beginning of the restoration of St. Edward's, although another five years went by before a concerted effort materialized. Meanwhile, the building continued to deteriorate, broken glass in the windows and leaks in the roof, exposed the interior to the elements. Water damage was extensive, particularly to plaster walls and ceilings.

It was the new rector, the Venerable Archdeacon A.W.L. Smith who rekindled the flame. No sooner had he been inducted, in 1916, than, "he straightway undertook the work with such commendable enterprise, energy and success as to completely restore rare Old St. Edward's inside and out". From then on, it became a labour of love for all those parishioners and members of the community who worked so faithfully with the rector. In his *History of the Old Church 1916-1937*, Archdeacon Smith recorded that "there was a strong public opinion in favour of restoring the Old Church", and he was quick to take advantage of this fact. Since there was little money, he built a model of the church, and, at a garden party held that summer of 1916, he sold off designated squares of the roof as a visual means of raising money and showing the donors where their money would be spent. The proceeds from this affair, together with other donations of money and voluntary labour, made it possible to tackle the most pressing job of making the roof tight, as well lighter work such as the re-installation of the pew doors. The authenticity of the restoration was important to the parishioners. For example, when only a few hand-made nails, with which fasten the pew doors, were found, a sample nail was sent to Brooklyn, New York, where the required number of handmade replicas were made. And all this was done long before authentic restoration became as popular as it is today.

The restoration must have made a startling transformation in the appearance of the old church, and undoubtedly, the transformation gave St. Edward's a new lease on life. Since then, a corps of devoted friends have provided the loving care necessary to maintain this significant example of early church architecture in Nova Scotia.

St. George's Round Church, Halifax

BRIDGE
P
STOP

Known by successive generations of Haligonians as the "Round Church", St. George's stands today as one of our esteemed landmarks, distinguished by its unique design, and steeped in a rich historical background.

St. George's history is an extension of the history of the Little Dutch Church, which served the parish from 1756 until it became too small to serve the growing community. Under the inspired leadership of Rev. Michael Houseal, who was rector from 1786 to 1799, a decision was made to build a new and larger church. The events leading to this decision are not too well documented, but by far the most important event was the arrival in Halifax of His Royal Highness Prince Edward, who was later to become the father of Queen Victoria. As Commander-in-Chief of his Majesty's Forces in Halifax, the Prince undoubtedly had many responsibilities and duties, but it was not long before he was displaying a special interest in the "German mission" on Brunswick Street. It would be logical to attribute this interest to his German ancestry, but in his own right, he was also something of an "amateur architect". This accounts for the very significant role he played in the seeking of funds and in the design of the new church.

It was following Prince Edward's return from England in 1798, where the title of Duke of Kent had been bestowed upon him, that he commissioned William Hughes, of H.M. Naval Yard, to prepare plans for the new church. It was the Duke's wish that St. George's be large enough to accommodate not only the growing congregation but also a portion of the growing garrison of troops. With this in mind, he had used his influence to obtain substantial grants from the British government and the provincial treasury. He had also returned with a handsome contribution from King George III. Hughes, a master shipwright by trade, set to work on the plans with the assistance of John Merrick, later to become the architect for Province House, and a Mr. J. Flieger who was a member of the congregation. They produced the unusual classical design "in the round" using a plan form reminiscent of the Byzantine basilicas which dated back to the time of the Crusades.

There is no clear evidence to establish who, in fact, designed the "Round Church". One might be inclined to give the credit to William Hughes, but the work might just as well be ascribed to Merrick. Whatever the case may be, it is quite apparent that the special architectural preferences of the Duke of Kent were meticulously adhered to. His predeliction for classical detail and architectural forms "in the round" was amply demonstrated in the design of St. George's, just as it was in the design of the Rotunda at Prince's Lodge on the shores of Bedford Basin, and the Old Town Clock on the eastern slope of Citadel Hill.

The death of Rev. Houseal on March 9, 1799, just as the congregation was ready to embark on the building of the new church, was a great shock to his faithful followers. But his successor, the Rev. George Wright, lost no time in picking up the loose ends. A lot was purchased at the northwest corner of Brunswick and Cornwallis Streets for the sum of £120 and on April 10, 1800, the cornerstone was laid by Governor John Wentworth "in the presence of the Commissioners and a number of respectable gentlemen." Although the Duke of Kent did not leave Halifax until August 3, 1800, he was not, for some reason, among the "respectable gentlemen" present on that occasion. In fact, it is ironical that having made such a remarkable contribution to the building of the church, he was destined never to worship there.

The first service was conducted by Rev. George Wright on July 19, 1801. The building was far from completed, for history records that a canvas covering was used to keep out the rain and snow for some time thereafter. The original building was finally completed in 1812, when a further sum of £500 was received from the Arms Fund. This helped materially to put the finishing touches to the main body of the church. There is an interesting watercolour which provides us with an excellent picture of the building at that time. The sketch shows the main body of the church very much as we see it today — a circular building 60 feet in diameter, two stories high at the outer wall, reducing to a

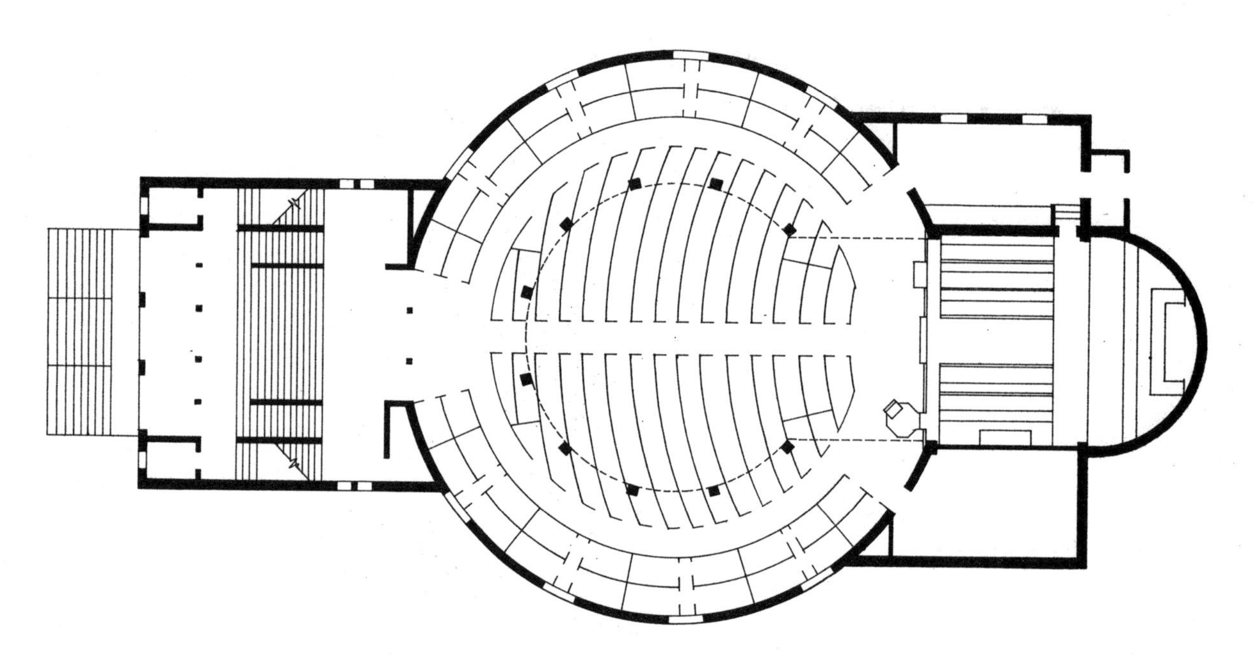

Plan

0 5 ft

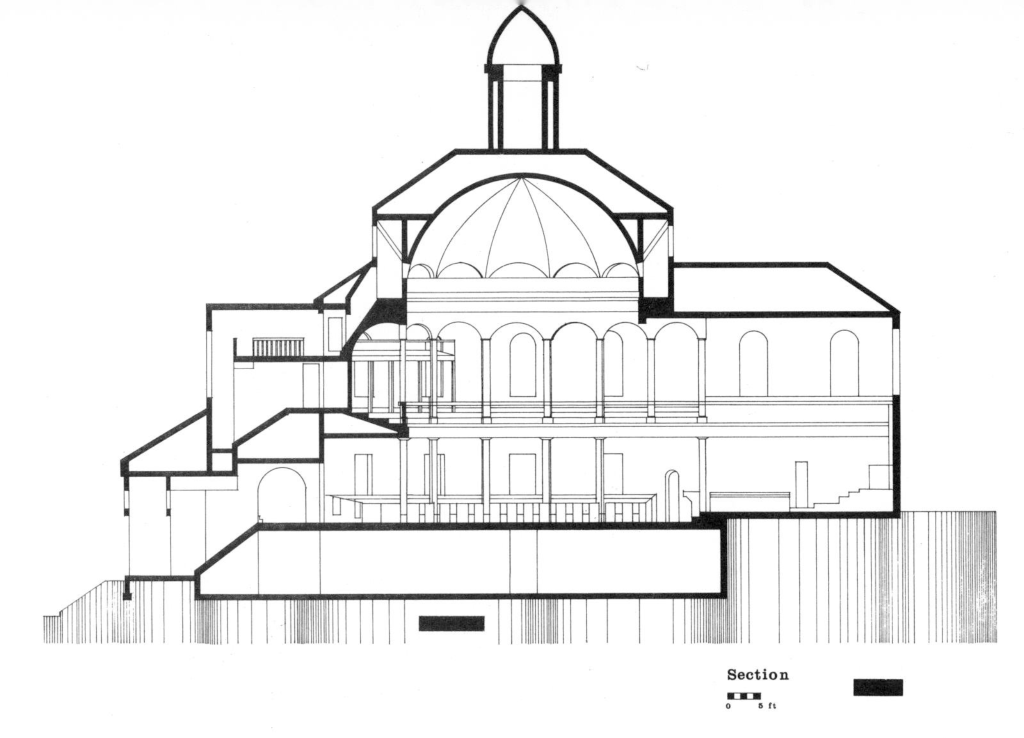

domed clearstorey, 35 feet in diameter, and reducing once again to a colonnaded cupola, with a dome. Today, the dome is topped by a gilded ball finial and weathervane.

The weathervane commemorates the prediction of the astronomer Halley, who, in 1760, discoverd the comet named after him, and predicted that it would re-appear in the skies 75 years later. The comet appeared in 1835, and excited much interest. Mr. Uniacke, the then rector, suggested that the new weathervane should commemorate the comet's reappearance, and it was so ordered.

St. George's circular plan form required a good deal of innovative timber framing, and this is particularly so in the framing for the main floor, where the large timber beams radiated out from the center, like the spokes of a great wheel, some 60 feet in diameter. Between the spokes, which were supported by stone foundations, burial vaults were provided. The only access to the vaults was by removing wedge-shaped sections of the floor.

The original building was strictly a circular building without appendages. The first major addition occurred in 1827, when the chancel, with its apsidal, semi-circular end was attached on the west side. At a later date, the chancel was flanked on either side with a vestry and organ chamber.

Prior to the building of the chancel, the pulpit was located in the center of the church with the altar occupying an elevated position against the curved wall on the west side where the gallery terminated. With the removal of the altar and pulpit to the new chancel, the interior of St. George's assumed its present day appearance.

The interior of the church has been well preserved and retains the arrangement of pews

originally installed. The sanctuary is circular, with a central aisle and two side aisles. Square wooden posts support a gallery that encircles three quarters of the sanctuary. Since it was the Duke of Kent's wish that this church be utilized as a church for the garrison, the front pews of the gallery were reserved for the officers. Higher still, fringing the dome, is another gallery fitted with crude, hard benches allotted to the slaves or servants who could follow the service looking through the segmented arch openings at the base of the domed ceiling. These original benches, showing the signs of years of wear, are still in place.

The other major change to St. George's occurred in 1911, when the earlier three storey, semi-circular entrance porch on Brunswick Street was replaced by the present square entrance porch, with its greatly increased stair access to the nave and galleries. Quite obviously this was a case where practical considerations overruled any argument that the original, semi-circular appendage was, from an architectural point of view, much more pleasing to the eye.

St. George's is a remarkable legacy in the area of Halifax that was once an early northern suburb of the original settlement. Brunswick Street later flourished as the fashionable residential area for the English speaking merchant families. Surviving modern pressures of neighbourhood re-development, St. George's today is a monument to the past and an inspiration for the present generation.

Old
Covenanter Church,
Grand Pré

The Covenanter Church at Grand Pré is the oldest, existing Presbyterian church in Nova Scotia. The church derives its name from those Presbyterians known as "Covenanters", who adhered sternly to doctrinal standards and a strict interpretation of the Covenant with the Sovereign. However, when construction of the church began in 1804, the congregation chose to erect a building which was a faithful reproduction of the traditional New England meeting house; it was the very embodiment of the Congregationalist spirit.

This is not surprising, for when the Rev. James Murdoch arrived in Grand Pré in 1766, he recruited his first congregation from among the New England "Planters", many of whom were Congregationalists. Murdoch was the first Presbyterian minister to settle permanently in the province. He had been sent out by the General Associate Synod of Ulster in response to an urgent cry for ministers "to preach the Gospel to the rapidly perishing Redmen". However, this was not to be, for he quickly discovered that the Micmac Indians of Nova Scotia had already been converted by the Roman Catholic missionaries.

The story of the Old Covenanter Church began with Governor Lawrence's Proclamation of 1759, which set in motion the tide of migration towards Nova Scotia. This proclamation guaranteed full liberty of conscience to Protestant settlers in the province. So it was that a large contingent of Planters set sail aboard 22 transports to settle in the land of the Acadians. History records the fact that they landed at Horton on June 4, 1760, "where the Cornwallis River flows into Minas Basin". With a grant of 100 acres to each settler and 50 acres to each member of the family, the settlers were under obligation to cultivate their holding within 30 years.

These were difficult times for the new settlers of Horton and Grand Pré. Years of conflict between the French and English, and the vacuum caused by the expulsion of the Acadians, had cast a shadow over the land. This was the situation that faced the Rev. James Murdoch when he came to Horton and settled on "a full 500 acre grant of dikeland, upland and woodland". In that first year, Murdoch gathered together a small group of Planters and, on a piece of his own "Planter Allotment", north of the Grand Pré-Hortonville Road, they built their first church building out of logs.

When Murdoch accepted a call to Meagher's Grant in 1791, his place was taken by the Rev. George Gilmore, who, like Murdoch, was a graduate of the School of Theology of the University of Edinburgh. By 1791, the old log church building was showing signs of serious deterioration which led finally to its demolition in 1795. There seems to be no explanation for the nine years that elapsed before the congregation started to build the present church, nor is there any reference to where the congregation worshipped during that period of time. However, it is reasonable to assume that the manse served this purpose.

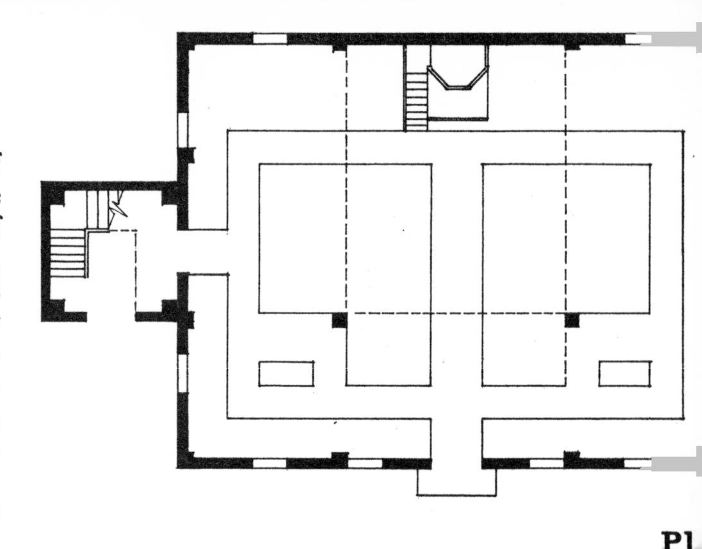

One might have expected that 37 years of Presbyterianism under Murdoch and Gilmore would have erased the last vestige of Congregational influence. Certainly by 1811, when the main body of the new building was complete, Congregationalism as practiced by those early New England settlers had ceased to flourish. For those members of the church who still had Congregationalist leanings, there was an unwritten agreement with the Presbyterians that the hymns of the Congregationalist Minister, Isaac Watt, would continue to be sung.

Traditionally, the 18th century Congregational meeting house was a plain and austere building, simple in plan and spare in detail. Yet, it had a certain beauty due in no small measure to its overall simplicity and symmetry of design. The Covenanter Church was in this tradition, having the usual rectangular floor plan, with the three-sided gallery, and the high, three-decker pulpit directly opposite the main entrance. Similarly, the double range of well-proportioned windows were symmetrically arranged in five bays on the front and rear elevation, and three bays on the ends.

The Covenanter Church possessed an additional measure of refinement, something that has been referred to as "a thin veneer of British classicism". This was evident in the use of a classical entablature supported by pilasters at the main entrance, a refinement that could well be attributed to the influence of the more style-conscious Loyalists who had arrived on the scene in the 1780's.

Until the tower was added at the south end, the building had no distinguishing features to identify it as a church. In outward appearance, it could quite easily be taken for a plain, and nicely proportioned, 18th century Georgian house. However, when the tower, belfry and steeple were completed in 1818, a transformation occurred. The Covenanter Church became the beautiful country "kirk on the hill", that we know today; it is a reminder of the Congregationalist Church in Nova Scotia, and one of our most cherished landmarks.

Undoubtedly, it is the design and detail of the tower, belfry and steeple that is the real eye-catcher, aided and abetted by its beautiful setting in a tree-surrounded country churchyard. The tall, slender proportions of the ten-foot square tower is particularly pleasing, and is complimented by the muntined

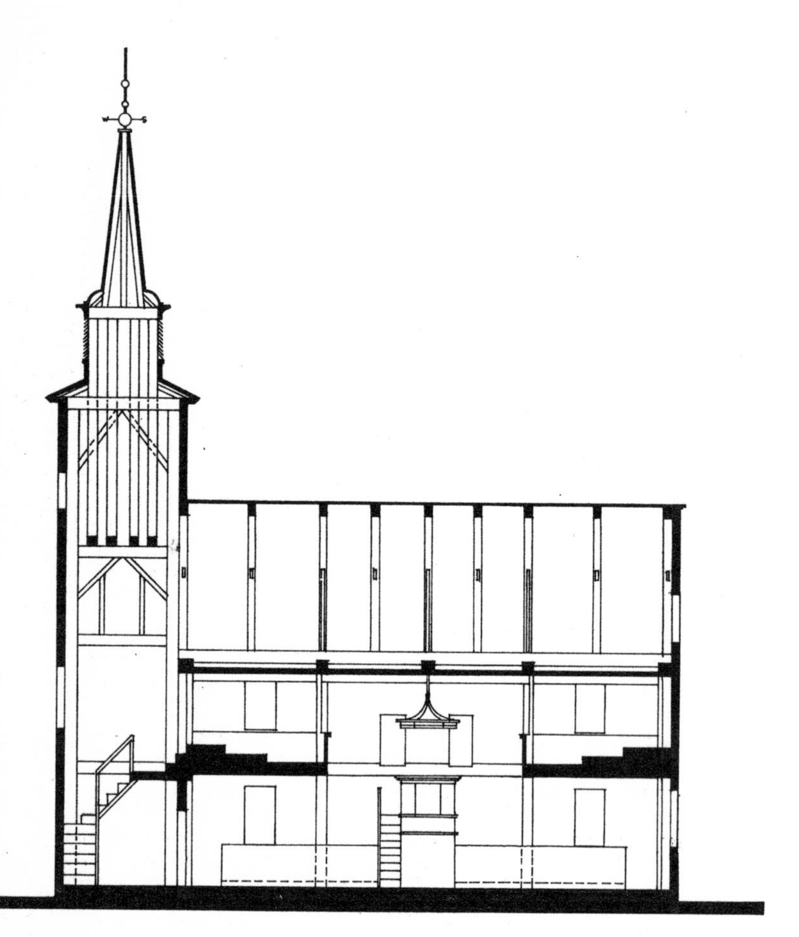

Section

window at the second floor level, and the rondel window above. A simple cornice and low roof transition leads the eye to the eight round-headed, louvred openings of the octagonal belfry with its domed roof, and upwards to the slender, octagonal spire, and the three-ball metal finial, with cardinal points and arrow weathervane.

As pleasing as one may consider the exterior of the church, the interior of the old meeting house also sets it apart as one of our treasured landmarks. In keeping with the traditional liturgical emphasis that Protestants placed on the spoken word, the three-tiered pulpit became the centrepiece of the New England meeting house; the pulpit, of course, is the dominant feature that greets the eye as one enters Old Covenanter's through the front door.

Centered on the long wall opposite the entrance, and approached by the relatively short aisle leading across the width of the building, the pulpit takes on a special significance. Not only is it a very fine piece of craftsmanship, but it also performs several important functions in the conduct of the Presbyterian service.

The lowest level consisted of a desk with seats and wide shelves for the necessary books. A clerk might occupy this place, recording attendance, and attending to other congregational matters. Or, as was the practice in a Presbyterian service, this area might be occupied by a "Precentor" who would "line out" the hymns and lead the service of praise,

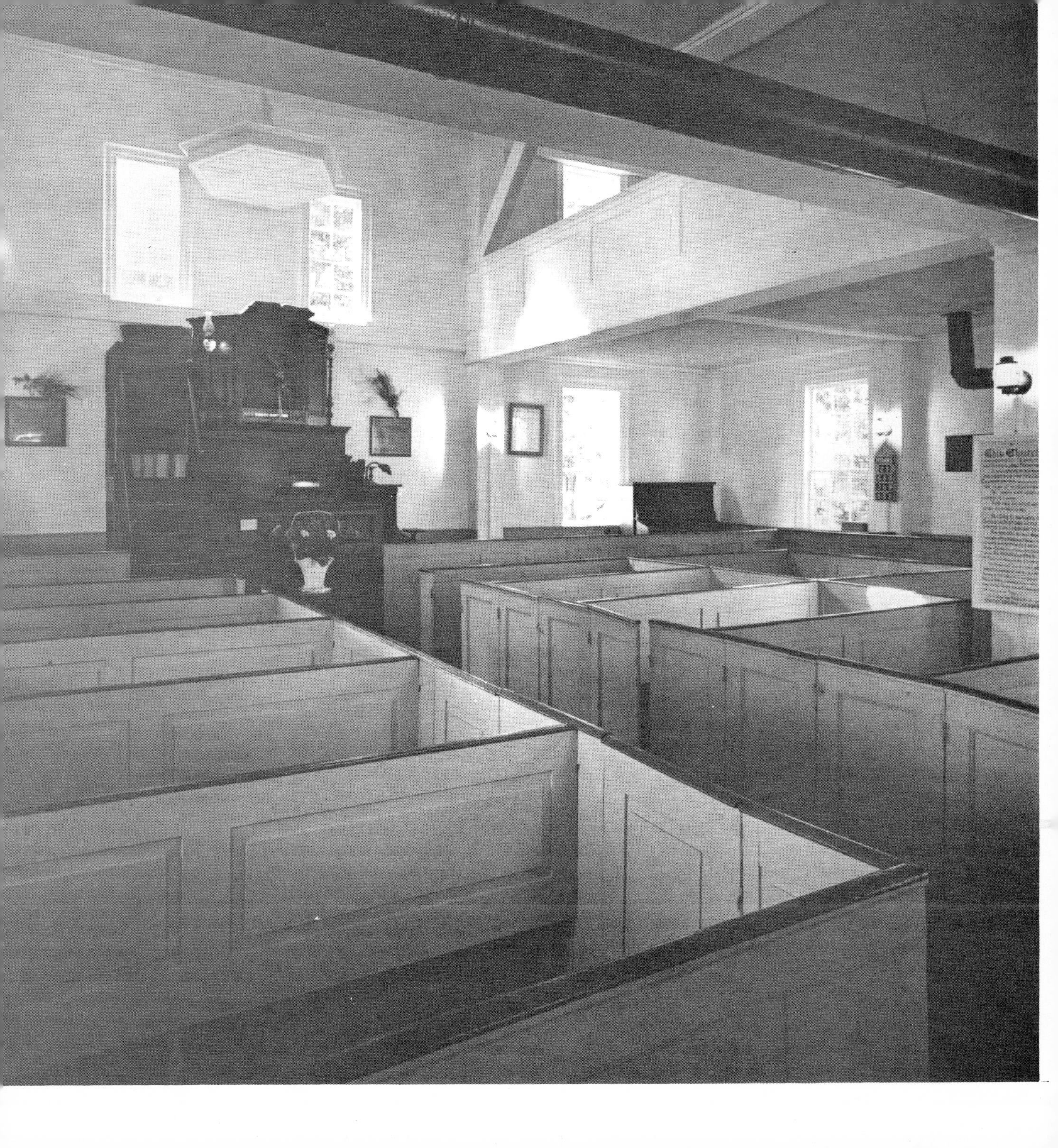

sometimes assisted by one or two others. It became known as the "Precentor's Box". The second tier was the "Lectern platform" two or three steps above the main floor with a panelled front and lectern from which the Scripture would be read. Finally the third tier, up another seven steps or so, was the pulpit or "preaching stand" enclosed with a five-sided, panelled front, one side being a hinged gate. Long-stemmed oil lamps were placed on the pulpit, and sometimes an hour glass measured the length of the sermon.

The Old Covenanter Church is one of the few remaining churches in the Maritimes to have its original, three-tiered pulpit intact. Also intact above the pulpit is the genuine, octagonal sounding board which was used to project the reading of the gospel and the preaching of the sermon. The sounding board is said to amplify sound as adequately as any electronic equipment. The old, square and rectangular box pews with moulded detailing are just as they were in pioneer times.

Today, the Covenanter Church is owned by the United Church of Canada. It is not open regularly throughout the year, but still draws summer congregations, mostly made up of visitors to the region. And to come to the Covenanter Church on a summer's day, to sit where countless congregations have sat, to cast one's eyes up to the high pulpit or to look through the antique window panes, is to feel the strength of those threads of tradition that our ancestors brought to this pioneer land.

Church of St. John, Cornwallis

The Church of Saint John embellishes the serene, pastoral landscape of Cornwallis township in the Annapolis Valley. The church, with its lofty, classical spire, is the distinguished legacy of the anglophone colonists, just as the landscape is the distinguished legacy of the Acadians who wisely reclaimed the fertile meadows from the tides of the Bay of Fundy. After the merciless expulsion of the Acadians in 1755, their undulating dykelands lay fallow for five years. Then, in June of 1760, the new colonists came. More than twenty vessels brought the settlers from the New England colonies of Connecticut and Rhode Island to Cornwallis and its neighbouring townships.

The majority of the newcomers were not initially Anglicans. In fact, they were divided into many sects. While there was no resident Anglican clergyman in the area at that time, the Rev. Dr. Breynton of St. Paul's in Halifax travelled out occasionally to preach and baptize children. Also, in 1761, the Rev. Joseph Bennett was officially appointed as missionary to the district by the Society for the Propagation of the Gospel on the recommendation of the Governor.

The early services of Cornwallis were held "in the most convenient houses and barns", and it was not until the arrival of John Burbidge, that a place of worship was envisaged. Burbidge, a former British military man and member of Nova Scotia's House of Assembly, came from Halifax in 1762 to settle. He, along with a handful of men in the vicinity, organized the parish. Then, Burbidge donated an acre of land and, with the help of his friend William Best, built a small primitive church building. This building, while never formally consecrated, was used for almost half a century and finally sold at auction in 1814 for £14, 5s. Local tradition maintains that the small structure was later re-sold, moved from its original foundation, and is still in use as an out-building on a farm just down the road from the present Church of Saint John.

John Burbidge, or Colonel Burbidge after his appointment to the militia, played an even more significant role, though less active, in the construction of the new church. At the annual meeting of the parish on September 29, 1802, the gathered brethren unanimously agreed to build a new church, and a committee was formed "to determine on the spot whereon to build the new church". At the same meeting, Col. Burbidge, then aged 86 years, retired from the office of Church Warden. He had pledged £100 towards the construction of the new church and an additional £50 if a spire was erected according to his plans. One can safely assume that the unique and beautiful spire that completes the church today was exactly the style that Col. Burbidge had wanted. For he lived to the age of 95 years, long enough to see the new church and spire accomplished.

A new site was chosen on the Glebe Farm, which was about one mile from the old church. Construction began in 1804 when a large gathering of men from all parts of the township raised the frame; many women were also

present and busy providing refreshments for the workers. The frame was clad with clapboard and the roof covered that year. Great care was taken in constructing the steeple. The square, saddle-back tower which would form the base, was built but left open; the delicately-detailed, slender spire was then built inside the tower with its posts resting on the floor. Four years later, on December 5, 1808, the feat of raising the spire was achieved with a good deal of ingenuity and co-operation. Several large sailing ships (Brigs of the West India trade) were in port nearby; sturdy, marine hoisting gear and crew members were borrowed from the visiting vessels. At another gathering of men, the spire was hoisted into place above the square tower, and secured firmly for the years to come.

Due to lack of funds, the interior was not completed until 1812, though the church was formally opened on Christmas Day, in 1810. The total cost of construction was $10,000 of which more than $7,000 was subscribed by the parishioners. In fact, the parishioners were so eager and determined to complete their beautiful church that they were willing to risk personal financial ruin. Bishop Charles Inglis related such a case in a letter to Governor Sir George Prevost in 1811. The Bishop told of a zealous church warden who had made himself solely responsible for an outstanding debt in excess of £500. The creditors were pressing for payment, and the warden was faced with the threat of losing his own property. His fellow parishioners could not help, having already subscribed their utmost. Fortunately, the Governor responded favourably to the Bishop's sad tale of the warden's debt. The sum of £500 was granted by the Governor to the Church of Saint John from the Arms Fund.

The exterior appearance of the church epitomizes the blending of British classical style and local pioneer materials. Like the great churches of Georgian England, classical detail abounds. There is, for example, a splendid Palladian window at the east or chancel end of the building, while at the west end, the main entrance is ornamented by a superb semi-circular fan light, Georgian pediment and side pilasters. The doorway is flanked on either side by a long, round-headed arch window with decorative keystones and moulding trim. Three similarly-styled windows are placed along the north and south walls, and corner pilasters add a finishing

touch. The magnificent steeple is the crowning achievement; it is modelled on those created by Sir Christopher Wren. It is not surprising that Col. Burbidge remembered the greatest spires of his homeland, and hoped to build a facsimile in the new country he was helping to shape.

The base of the steeple is a square tower displaying on each side a decorative circular window and corner pilasters. The shingled roof forms a bellcast flair and a pattern of triangles where it attaches itself to the lantern above. The intricately-detailed lantern is octagonal in shape with open keystone arches through which one can easily see the large bell. The lantern is topped by a rounded octagonal cap which is in turn surmounted by a slender, octagonal spire with a handsome brass weathervane.

The overall effect is awesome. While the classical details and graceful spire lend majestic dignity to the church, the materials, wood and shingle, add a lightness and simplicity which the great stone churches of Britain would not have had.

The interior of the church is not in its original plain or stark condition, and has an air of being well kept up over the years. The eye of the observer is greeted by an expanse of varnished wood: the rounded ceiling is covered in varnished diagonal wood strips with exposed varnished beams; ornamental varnished columns, and richly moulded wood wainscotting, probably a Victorian addition, decorate the walls of the nave; a wide, varnished keystone arch with reeded side pilasters leads to the chancel where the wainscotting, ceiling, and window-surrounds are all of varnished wood. The original rectangular, box-style pews are still in use though they were re-arranged in 1888 to create a centre aisle. Probably at that time, too, the doors were removed to give the pews a more up-to-date appearance. Other notable features include the wide floorboards, still unfinished in the gallery, and the heavy, primitive construction. The huge, hand-hewn beams which may be seen in the belfry are approximately 16 by 16 inches. Square wooden pegs and hand-wrought nails are also in evidence.

A number of changes have occurred during the church's history. Perhaps the most significant change took place in 1869, when a vestry was added and the chancel was lengthened by ten feet to accommodate the

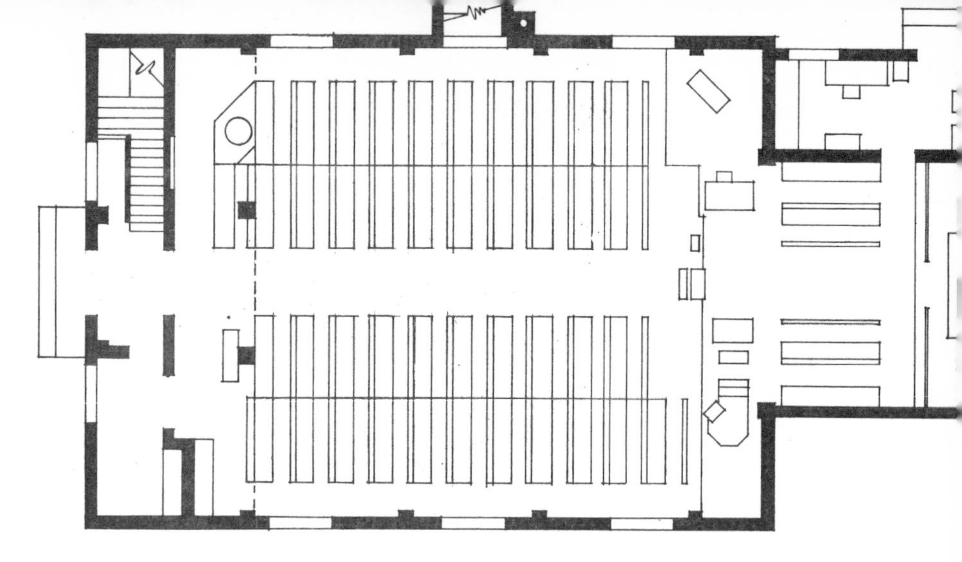

choir pews. Fortunately, these structural renovations were carried out with great care and have not detracted noticeably from the classical proportions of the building. The church was heated by wood stoves until a small room was dug out underneath to house a furnace. The original oil lamps were replaced by an acetylene system in 1909, and by electricity in 1921.

Today, the Church of Saint John flourishes, with a resident minister and a large congregation. One can imagine that the settlers of long ago who gave their hard-earned money and who gathered in the spirit of co-operation to raise the frame and hoist the spire, would be well pleased to know that their church is still used by their descendants and appreciated as one of the finest historical landmarks of the province.

Goat Island Church

The Goat Island Baptist Church is not, as its name suggests, situated on Goat Island. Rather, it is located on the main route between Annapolis Royal and Digby overlooking Goat Island in the Annapolis Basin.

The origin of the Goat Island Baptist Church dates back to the evangelistic fervor of the New Light Movement which came with the early Puritan settlers from New England.

Numerous revivals were held in Annapolis County as the Movement "swept over the country with the force and fury of a torrent". One such revival took place at Clements in March, 1810, and resulted in the founding of the Goat Island Church.

The man who was the most instrumental in the revival was Israel Potter. He had been born in Massachusetts in 1763, before his family emigrated to Nova Scotia. At the age of 17, he served in the Second Massachusetts Regiment during the American Revolution. When peace was declared, he moved to his father's homestead at Clements in Annapolis County; there his pursuits included farming, fishing, brickmaking, lumbering and vessel-building. After his marriage, he resided across the Basin in Lower Granville (Karsdale) where he was converted and baptized. In 1810, just before the revival, he settled with his family in the old Potter homestead at Clements.

On May 12, 1810, Israel Potter wrote to the editor of the *Herald of Light* in Springfield, Massachusetts, describing the revival and its results. "In the beginning of March last, a most wonderful and powerful reformation began in the lower part of this town, which seemed to prevade the minds of old and young, and many, we hope, were brought to the knowledge of the truth. About ten days afterwards the good work made its appearance in the middle of town. The people assembled from every quarter, and it seemed that it might be truly said that God was passing through the place in a very powerful manner. The glorious work has since spread through every part of the town, and some of all ages have been made to bow to the mild sceptre of the Redeemer.

"The ordinance of baptism has been administered for five Sabbaths successively. Forty-five have been admitted to this sacred rite, and a church has been constituted upon the gospel plan, consisting of sixty-five members, to which we expect further additions. If I should say that 200 have been hopefully converted to the Lord in this town since the reformation commenced, I think I should not exceed the truth. The good work is still spreading eastward very rapidly, and looks likely to spread through the province."

At first, the newly formed church met in the kitchen of the old Potter homestead where "the preaching, the exhortation, the old songs of Zion, the shouting of the saints..." were part of those early services. It is probable that construction began on the Meeting House, as it was called, in late 1810 or early 1811. This date gives Goat Island Church the distinction of being the oldest existing Baptist church in Nova Scotia. The distinction is well-deserved, for incredible as it may seem, the church has had very few changes, and today, is very much as it was in the days of Israel Potter and the first congregation.

Strangely, though, if one set out to look for the oldest Baptist church in the province, one would be more likely to notice the North West Range Meeting House, than the Goat Island Church. The reason is that most of the early Baptist churches were built in the plain, rectangular "meeting house" style with equally plain square or rectangular windows; they, in fact, looked more like houses than churches. Goat Island Church, on the other hand, is very definitely constructed in an ecclesiastical style with a prominent steeple and an array of gothic windows. While the steeple is not original, the aged, hand-hewn beams of its construction indicate that it was added only a few years after the main body of the church was built.

The design elements may have been influenced by other churches of the area, notably the Anglican Christ Church which was built at Karsdale in 1791. For example, the slim, gothic windows of the Goat Island Church are very similar to those of Christ Church with almost identical mouldings around the window arches. Christ Church, too, has a square steeple capped by a pointed roof, though the Goat Island steeple is of larger proportions and a grander style. The Goat Island Church has a clapboard exterior as does Christ Church, but has more elaborate pilaster trim at the corners.

The explanation for the design influence of a church of another denomination is not difficult to understand. Geographically, the Goat Island Church is situated almost directly across the Annapolis Basin from Karsdale which suggests that some of the builders may have come across to help with the building of the Goat Island Church. As well, Israel Potter, the leading figure in the organization of the Goat Island Church, spent the early years of his married life in Karsdale and was presumably very familiar with the appearance of Christ Church. Thus, it is not surprising that the Goat Island Church shared some of the characteristics of its neighbour.

However, whatever theories may be postulated about the exterior design of the church, it is, without a doubt, the interior which is truly remarkable. When the enormous brass key is turned in the lock and the heavy, original, double doors creak open, one steps into the early 19th Century.

Flanking the side aisles are the large, square box pews where the worshippers would sit around on three sides so that each could see the preacher and concentrate on the sermon. In the centre, are the rows of rectangular box pews where the worshippers would all sit facing forward to the pulpit. Placed at intervals along the edges of the pew boxes are eight gracefully turned candle holders, each 24 inches high. And along the front of the gallery an additional five long-stemmed, metal candle holders curve outwards and upwards to aid those sitting in the smaller box pews which fill the gallery.

Sometime after the invention of kerosene in the 1840's, a "new-fangled" light fixture, a stylish chandelier with four oil lamps, was hung from the centre of the ceiling. Fortunately, the advent of electricity in this century, caused no such change, for, to this day, no electricity has been brought to Goat Island Church, though the power lines pass close by on the road outside.

Each of the pew doors, which kept the chill draughts from the feet of our forebears, is decorated with mouldings in a dignified square pattern. The repeated pattern of squares also embellishes the front of the gallery. While the pews, like the wide pine floorboards, are painted grey, the pew doors as well as the front of the gallery are 'grained' as was the fashion in the late 19th century.

Other items of interest in the pioneer church are: the small foot-pump organ with "mouse-proof pedals", the marble plaque to Israel Potter and a frail Bible, dated 1859 which belonged to his descendant, James Potter. Also, there are two long-handled collection boxes still ready for use, and two "Iron King" wood stoves, cast at a Windsor, Nova Scotia, foundry, which add a certain practical charm.

For the more avid historian or architect, the upper reaches of building also prove very enlightening. Access is through a narrow trap door in the ceiling above the gallery. One may view the incredibly rugged construction. Although the building is fast approaching the end of its second century in age, a look at its solid structure would convince even the most skeptical that it will last for centuries to come. Of particular note, are the two rough-hewn "ship's knees", still partly covered with bark, that brace the front corner posts of the frame.

Today, Goat Island Baptist Church is part of the Deep Brook United Baptist Pastorate, along with three other churches in the area. While services are not held in the church regularly throughout the year, occasional services are held there during the warmer summer months, and every year, a special memorial service is performed in August. And, not long ago, the wedding of Elizabeth Potter, a descendant of Israel Potter, filled the historic church with candlelight and joyous voices, continuing the customs begun almost two centuries ago.

All Saints',
Granville Centre

All Saints' Anglican Church at Granville Centre is a wayside church. Situated on a promontory of land, the small church with its graceful spire is a landmark on the main road through the fertile farmland of the Annapolis Valley. To the west, stretches the North Mountain ridge; to the east, is the placid Annapolis River and far across the broad floor of the valley, the South Mountain ridge.

Because of the serene beauty of the landscape and the richness of the soil, it is not surprising that this area was the first to be permanently settled in the province. And with settlers, especially god-fearing farm folk, there came a need for a place of worship. Yet, the accomplishment of building a church was not without difficulty.

By September of 1789, Bishop Charles Inglis had visited Middle Granville as it was then called, and he had recommended that a church should be built on the site that had already been set aside for it. Two years later in 1791, when the Bishop returned to the district, he found that while the frame of the church had been raised and covered in, the building was still an unfinished shell.

Evidently, no further attempt was made to complete the church. By 1811, a full decade later, the situation had become more desperate. In a report to the Governor, Bishop Inglis explained the problem: "The church in the middle district is in a very unfinished state. It is considered so much larger than is necessary and is so much in decay that the congregation are very desirous of taking it down and completing a neat building of smaller dimensions."

Wisely, Bishop Inglis thought of a solution so that the people of Middle Granville could start afresh and build the small, neat church they wanted. He made a proposal to the Governor for a special grant suggesting that the money be taken from the Arms Fund. Bishop Inglis indicated that the total cost of the project would be approximately £500 and that the people, who were of moderate means, could raise £170. He hoped that the balance could be made up in the form of a grant.

The Governor, at that time, was Sir George Prevost, whose interests were not centered on the domestic or spiritual affairs of the province. He was a military man, a former army Major-General and Commander-in-Chief of the forces in Nova Scotia; one of his main achievements was the re-organization of the province's militia. In spite of his penchant for military matters, however, Governor Prevost acceded to the Bishop's request and duly granted £330 from his Arms Fund for the building of a small church in the lush farming district of the valley.

Thus, the deed was finally accomplished; the first unfinished church was replaced by the compact one we know today. Rev. John Milledge, who was rector from 1801 to 1817, was the overseer of the change. By 1814, he reported to the Society for the Propagation of the Gospel that the exterior would soon be finished. His successor, the Rev. George Best, nevertheless reported, in 1819, that the church was still incomplete and that "there is a large sum to be drawn for it still from this Province". The grant had, apparently, not been used up at that point. However, by February, 1821, Rev. Best seemed well satisfied when he wrote, "We are making every preparation towards completing our middle church, and I hope ere many months have passed, it will be in a fit state for Divine service." And, having been completely finished, All Saints' Church was consecrated in 1826.

While the saga of construction may have taken some years, the product is very definitely a fine example of church architecture. The overall proportions, though small, are classical in form. The exterior detailing, too, is classical or Georgian. There are round-headed or Romanesque arched windows, with keystone and pilaster detail fashioned in the wooden window mouldings. There is unmistakeable classical symmetry in the front elevation where two arched windows flank either side of the main door which is, itself, a round-headed arch surrounded by pilaster detailing and surmounted by a Georgian pediment. The cladding is clapboard, trimmed with pilasters at the corners.

The steeple, like those of St. Mary's at Auburn and St. John's at Cornwallis, is reminiscent of the elegant spires designed by the great architect of British classicism, Sir Christopher Wren. The saddle-back belfry is topped by a lantern and a long, slim spire with brass balls and weathervane at the pinnacle.

The interior of the church, which has

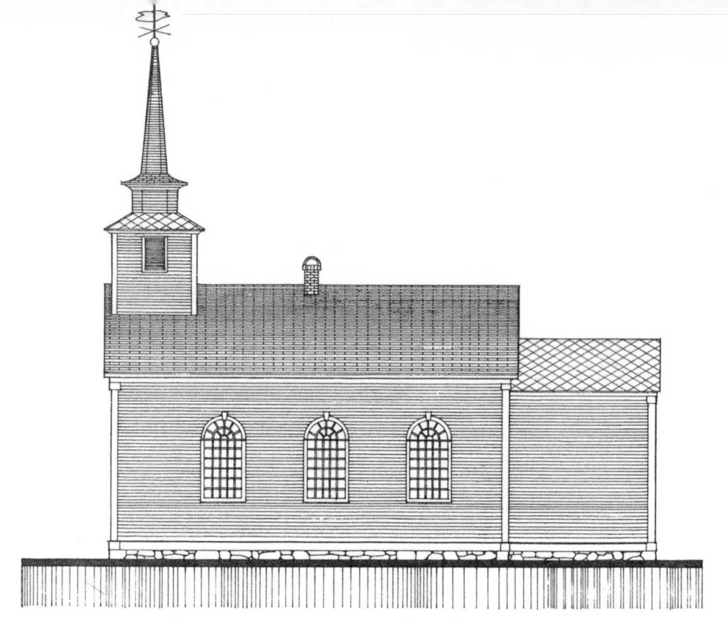
South Elevation

recently been extensively renovated, is very striking. The classic beauty of the arched windows is highlighted against the bare white walls; the grooved keystone and pilaster decoration around the windows, as well as the interior louvered shutters, are painted light grey. A thick, brilliant red carpet covering the centre aisle and the chancel add the warmth and richness of colour. But perhaps the most striking interior feature is the three magnificent gilt, kerosene-lamp chandeliers which have been unobtrusively wired for electricity. Also, a converted aladdin lamp hangs near the pulpit.

Over the years, various changes have been made to the interior of All Saints'. For the centenary in 1914, stained glass was added to the chancel window. In the 1940's, hardwood floors were laid in the nave, and probably about that time, the old pews with doors were exchanged for new, oak ones. The original pine floorboards and a couple of remnants of primitive benches may still be seen in the gallery which is now closed in, and contains the hot air heating system.

By gaining access to the belfry, via the trap door in the gallery and a ladder, the sturdy construction of hand-hewn, pegged beams may be readily observed. As well, there is the large, mellow-toned bell with a special toller on the side for funerals. The bell, about two feet in diameter and three feet high, bears the inscription, "Presented by the Ladies Knitting Circle 1885". Also marked on the bell is its place of origin, the Buckeye Bell Foundry of Cincinatti.

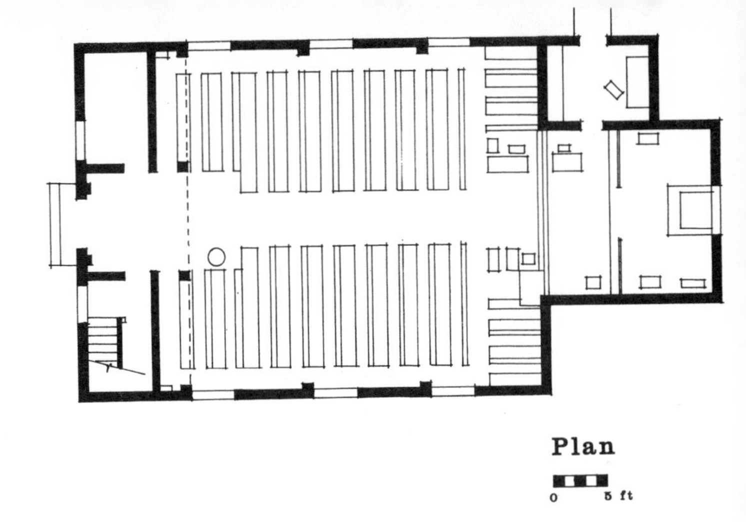

Plan

0 5 ft

A further change to the church may be noted while inside the belfry. The belfry has one small round-headed window on one side and rectangular louvered openings on the remaining three sides. It is most probable that the other three windows, which are still stored in the belfry, were replaced when the bell was installed in 1885.

In the most recent renovations of the nave, the plaster walls were redone with plasterboard, and the wide wainscotting was either removed or covered over. This was done when a number of the wide wainscotting "boards" turned out to be just plaster, while in other instances, the wainscotting was, in fact, all there was to the wall.

Like many other churches, the congregation of All Saints' has diminished in number. However, the congregation has amalgamated with those of Christ Church at Karsdale and St. Luke's in Annapolis Royal. Divine service is held at All Saints' about once a month and, as is now the custom, it is not merely the rector that is itinerant — it is the whole congregation too!

One of the special services of the year is held in each of the churches. It is fitting that every year the service for Thanksgiving is held at All Saints', just when the bountiful harvest of the valley is being gathered in all around.

St.Luke's, Annapolis Royal

St. Luke's, in Annapolis Royal, has its tradition in military history, and roots that go back to the year 1710 when the first Anglican service of thanksgiving was held in the chapel of the French fort of Port Royal after its capture by General Nicholson and his troops.

It was not, however, until 1784 that the first St. Luke's was constructed in Annapolis Royal while the Rev. Jacob Bailey was rector. By 1810, however, the church was in such a dilapidated condition that the members of the congregation petitioned the British government for a piece of land on which to construct a new house of worship. The British Government subsequently granted £500 and an acre of land on the southeast corner of White House Field which was situated directly across the road from Fort Anne. The land and grant were given on condition that a gallery in the Church would always be maintained for the use and accommodation "of such officers non-commissioned and soldiers in our service as shall be from time to time stationed and chartered in our fort or garrison at Annapolis".

Rev. Cyrus Perkins was chaplain to the King's forces in Annapolis Royal at this time, and it was during his tenure that tenders were called, in 1814, for a new church which became the present St. Luke's. Unfortunately, Rev. Perkins did not live to see completion of his church as he drowned accidently while vacationing in England in 1817.

The tender call for the new church included specific requirements. For example, the structure was to be 54 feet long by 36 feet wide and 23 feet high. A tower was to project six and one half feet out from the front of the structure, and each side was to contain one tier of five windows. Inside, the church was to have side and end galleries projecting six feet in width from the inner wall. The ceiling was to be arched overhead between the galleries, and the pulpit was to be finished according to the Corinthian order.

In 1815, the "raising" was held for the frame of the new church, but it was not until February 6, 1822, that the church was opened for service. By then, the Society for the Propagation of the Gospel had granted £400 towards its completion, and the total cost of construction was £1400. All the specifications seemed to have been met. The church was finished with one tier of five long, gothic windows on each side; the square tower was completed, although no belfry or spire had yet been added. In the interior, there were three galleries, one at each side and one at the west end facing the front of the nave. Above the galleries, the ceiling was flat but curved into a high, rounded arch between the galleries. And there was a three-decker pulpit finished in the Corinthian order.

In accordance with the original conditions of the government grant for the church, one side gallery was reserved exclusively for soldiers. Famous regiments sat here, such as the "Fighting 40th", the Highlanders with plumed hats, and also, soldiers who were later to be immortalized in Tennyson's "Charge of the Light Brigade". The officers, in the full

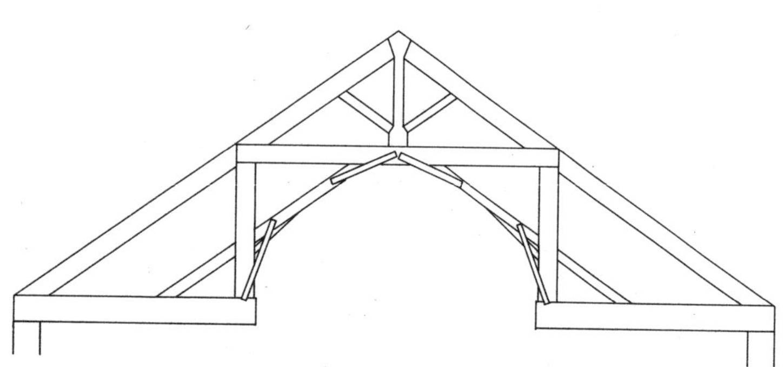

Roof Framing

regalia of bright uniforms, white trappings and black busbys, sat below in one of the box pews. In the opposite gallery, the front pews were rented by masters for their servants, some of whom were the black descendants of slaves. The end gallery or "singing gallery" accommodated the choir.

In 1837, the belfry and spire were finally added to the tower. The wide, octagonal belfry has louvered openings in the style of gothic arches, and on octagonal roof which sweeps up into a long, slim spire. The original weathervane, a dove with an olive branch in her mouth, was replaced by the present dart-shaped vane in 1850.

The major changes and Victorian "modernization" took place in the 1870's. For instance, in 1874, the side galleries were removed, probably because the military heyday was long since over, the garrison having been withdrawn in 1854. At the same time, the old box pews were replaced by new, oak bench-style pews which were fashionably decorated with a gothic arch motif. In 1879, the present chancel was added. In spite of the alterations, the interior is still interesting. There is high wainscotting made of wide, horizontal planks, and the original rough, unpolished, wide floorboards are readily visible. Under the high, arched ceiling, the "singing gallery" remains; an attractive, rounded arch with keystone and side pilasters decorates the wall behind.

In 1910, the congregation of St. Luke's celebrated the bicentenary of that first Anglican service held in the chapel at Port Royal. To commemorate the event, King George V sent over, with the Bishop of London, a magnificent prayer book. The King's Prayer Book, measuring 19 by 21 inches, is bound in red Morocco leather with heavy gold tooling and is encrusted with amethysts. When it was discovered that His Majesty had not autographed the book, it was sent back to England and later returned to Annapolis Royal with the royal signature on the fly leaf. The King's Prayer Book, which is truly unique, and can never be reproduced, may be seen by visitors to the church.

Today epauletted young men no longer promenade the streets, and the military band no longer escorts the officers and soldiers of the

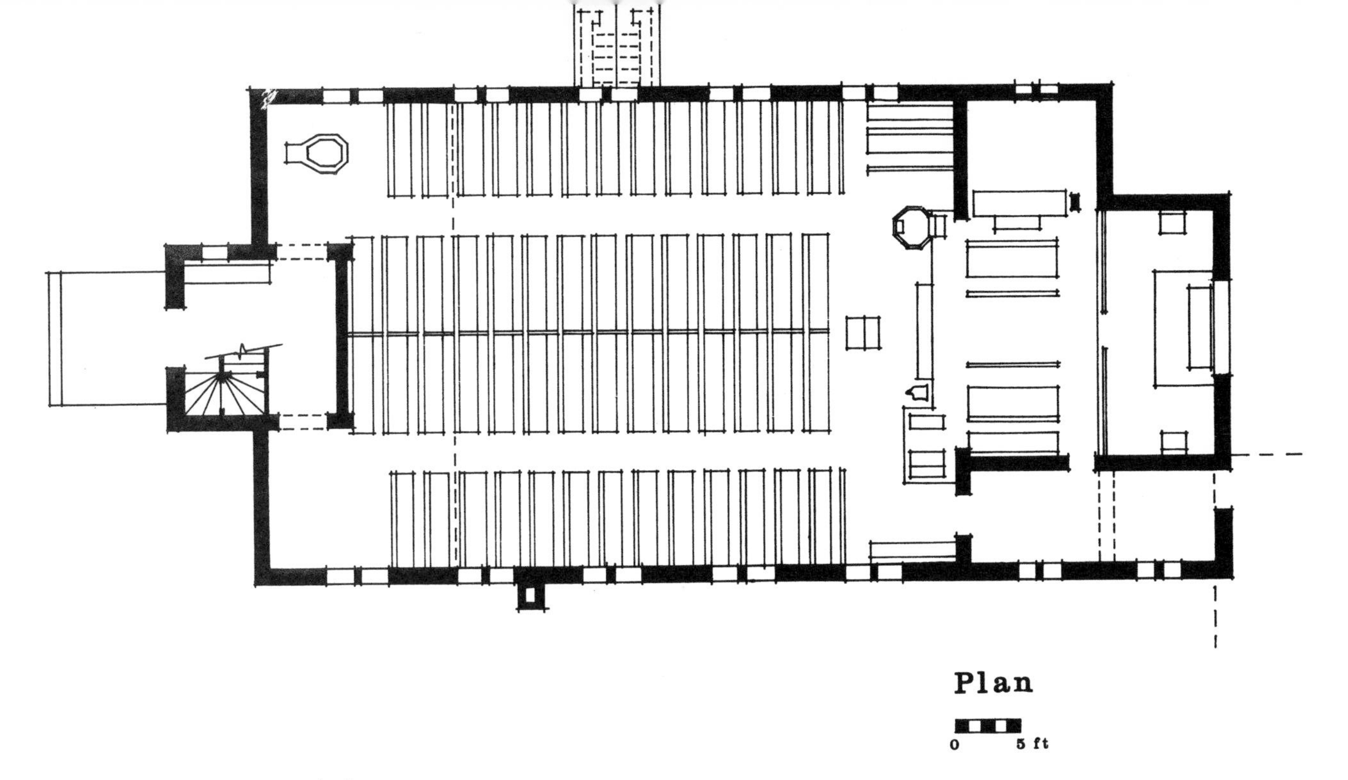

Plan

garrison to and from church on a Sunday morning. And yet, St. Luke's, the garrison church, remains, no longer in a field, but on the main street of the quiet, historic town of Annapolis Royal.

Christ Church, Dartmouth

In 1816, inhabitants of Dartmouth petitioned the Governor of Nova Scotia for financial aid to construct a church on a lot of land already granted for the purpose. The establishment of Christ Church Anglican was, at last, underway, 67 years after the founding of Dartmouth.

In 1750, the arrival of the "Alderney" had brought the first 353 settlers. Their spiritual needs were attended to by Rev. William Tutty of St. Paul's Church, Halifax, who crossed the harbour regularly to give open-air services. This practice was interrupted, when in May 1751, an Indian raid and massacre took place in the new settlement of Dartmouth. After 1785, a Quaker meeting house was built by newly-arrived settlers from Nantucket, Massachusetts, who had come to carry on their whaling industry in Dartmouth Cove. In 1792, St. John's Church was built at Preston, about seven miles away, in the middle of the vast parish which included Dartmouth. But it was not until July 9, 1817, that the cornerstone of Christ Church was laid by Sir John C. Sherbrooke, Earl of Dalhousie and Governor of Nova Scotia.

A note on the original plans states that Mr. Blaiklock was the builder. The basic style of the church is Georgian, or colonial Georgian, reminiscent of St. Paul's in Halifax. However, Christ Church is of a later vintage, and hence, was more elaborate in its original state. The transepts, while not as large as they are today, were developed, as was the chancel extension, and these were decorated with ornate, corner pilasters, Palladian and round-headed windows. The pitched roof had an attractive bellcast flair with fluted cornice-work underneath. The slim, pointed steeple rose above the belfry decorated with classical pediments and round-headed arches. A superb brass weathervane graced the tip of the steeple as it does today.

Various colourful figures are associated with the early years of the history of the Church. The Hon. Michael Wallace, who donated the church bell in 1826, was a leading politician of the time. He was a member of the Legislative Assembly from 1785 to 1803, and later, became Provincial Treasurer. Samuel Albro, one of the first Church Wardens, was one of Dartmouth's early industrialists. He ran a nail mill, a bark mill and a large tannery. John P. Mott, who also served as Church Warden, was one of the wealthiest men in the province. He established a chocolate and soap factory in 1844, and was estimated to be worth three-quarters of a million dollars when he died in 1890.

The church has survived various alterations, the threat of demolition and the largest disaster in the history of the harbour.

In 1855, a committee was appointed to investigate the cost of adding twenty feet to the length of the church. A report of the investigation was finally approved in 1864, and by the following year, the chancel had been lengthened and transepts enlarged. The enlargement was, fortunately, in keeping with the Georgian style of the original structure.

Upon completion of the work, church officials conveyed to the contractor, Thomas Davidson, "the great satisfaction that he had given the congregation in the fulfilment of his contract in such a creditable and workmanlike manner". Architect for the project was Henry Elliot.

Considering the "great satisfaction" upon the enlargement of the building, it is surprising to find that, less than a decade later, demolition of the building and the sale of site were being proposed. At Easter, in 1872, a committee was set up to look into the relative costs of changes including "the cost of a new chancel, the cost of a new front and steeple and the cost of a new church, the probable amount to be realized from the sale of the land on which the church stands". One month later the committee brought forward estimates for the construction of a new church; they also reported that the present site, if divided into building lots, would bring $6,000. Church officials then agreed to take the necessary steps towards the building of a new church; approximately $5,000 was raised by subscription for the purpose. At a subsequent meeting, however, there was disagreement over the sale of the site with the majority opposed to "the sale of the lands on which the church now stands". Furthermore, it was conceded that sufficient funds could not be raised without the sale of the land. Accordingly, the drastic proposal for the demolition of the church was dropped and the building was given the chance to serve those generations of the next century.

It was early in the next century, that the very fabric of the church was to suffer its greatest blow. Just six months after the ceremony that marked the 100th anniversary of Christ Church, the explosion of December 6, 1917 devastated both Halifax and Dartmouth. The munitions' ship *Mont Blanc*, carrying 4,000 tons of T.N.T. collided in mid-harbour with the *Imo*, causing the largest, man-made explosion before Hiroshima. Christ Church, only two blocks from the harbour, was heavily damaged. Historian, C.W. Bayer said of the scene, "Broken stained glass windows, twisted frame work, fallen plaster and cracked, ruined chimneys made up the heart-breaking picture that confronted the congregation". In monetary terms, the damage was estimated at $8,115.00.

It is to the credit of church officials of the day that demolition plans were not revived, even though the church was in a vulnerable state of disrepair. Instead, the church was completely restored. During the course of the restoration, the chancel was again extended by 16 feet. The specifications for the repair and enlargement of the church were prepared by architect, R. A. Johnson, while J. W. Embree of Amherst was the contractor. Services finally resumed in Christ Church on the first Sunday of March, 1919.

The old box pews, once sold for £5 apiece, were replaced early in this century with modern pews made of solid oak. A number of stained glass windows were donated throughout the years, the latest being, appropriately, the head of Christ with radiating petal-shaped rays, for the round window over the main entrance. The front porch was enlarged, incorporating the Georgian-style door with fan light. As well, two doors were added, one on either side of the porch, replacing the two windows originally on the west façade

On February 1, 1928, during the morning worship service, a fire broke out beneath the church in one of the two partial basements where the furnaces were kept. Fortunately, disaster was averted; quick action on the part of the sexton and the fire department kept the fire confined to the small area.

In 1945, an accidental explosion at an ammunition magazine on the Dartmouth shore, caused considerable damage to the church. Four stained glass windows were broken, three beyond repair. The Palladian window above the altar, with panels depicting the Ascension, was carefully restored.

Today, Christ Church, which still serves a congregation of more than 500, stands serene, sheltered by mature trees planted more than a century ago by faithful parishioners.

North West Range
Meeting House

PARKER

The United Baptist Church at North West Range in Lunenburg County exists today as tangible proof of the dedicated work of Joseph Dimock and his staunch supporters.

Dimock was the first, native-born Baptist minister ordained in Canada, and a prominent founder of the faith in Nova Scotia. Born at Newport, he began his career as an itinerant preacher in 1790, at the age of 22. He travelled widely in Digby, Annapolis, Cumberland, Queens and Lunenburg counties. In 1793, he became pastor of the church at Chester, after the death of its founder Rev. John Seccombe. This appointment, however, did not prevent the young evangelist from continuing his missionary work in the surrounding area.

Often such missionary work was done in the face of much hardship. Travelling conditions were abysmal, especially in winter, and it was not uncommon that meetings were disrupted by rowdy, even dangerous, hecklers. Joseph Dimock wrote a vivid account of a treacherous meeting which took place on a stormy, winter evening in the small community of North West, situated about four miles from the town of Lunenburg.

When the mob of protestors appeared, "some had side arms, some sickles or any stick they could pick up". Dimock remained calm, and delivered his sermon above the tumult. At the close of the meeting, "the mob made a struggle to get in but was resolutely opposed". The uproar continued; the mob "declared that they would not leave the house without Dimock", and "females were much alarmed and some screamed". Snowballs were thrown, hitting Dimock and his fellow worshippers. Finally, the Magistrate, Col. John Creighton, intervened assuring the protestors that to disturb the worship service was "as bad as to disturb any of the churches in town".

In spite of the unruly nature of that early meeting in North West, Joseph Dimock continued to minister to its inhabitants, who were of "foreign protestant" stock. In 1809, a church was formally organized with seven male and three female members; a clerk was chosen and two deacons were ordained. While the deacons presided over regular meetings of worship, Rev. Dimock preformed baptism and communion services for the following eight years, until a pastor was secured in 1817.

At a meeting on September 10, 1818, not long after the appointment of the pastor, Rev. Robert Davis, the members of the congregation, now 41 in number, unanimously agreed that a place of worship should be built. Thus, each gave according to his means; a total of £204 was raised and dutifully expended on the construction of the meeting house. Two years later, on August 12, 1820, the congregation held the first recorded gathering in their new meeting house to elect trustees to oversee the property.

The structure itself, with a frame of spruce and hemlock, and clapboard cladding, fits into the plain "meeting house" style traditionally associated with the houses of worship of the Congregationalists from New England. However, there are interesting variations.

Unlike the Barrington Meeting House or the Covenanter Church at Grand Pré,the main entrance is not centered in one of the longer façades of the building; instead the main doorway is placed slightly off-centre in one of the shorter façades. Nor are the pews placed parallel to the length of the church but, as the main entrance dictates, are arranged parallel to the width of the building. Thus, the configuration of the North West Range Meeting House, with the nave longer than it is broad, conforms more to the usual church pattern than that of the earliest meeting houses.

Classical details, like the corner pilasters and the mouldings above the windows, emphasize the dignity of the structure. There are gothic touches too. A small lancet window, similar to those which decorate many early houses in the province, is found under the peaked roof above the main entrance. Inside, a large, gothic window is the backdrop for the pulpit; the translucent glass was, about 10 years ago, fitted into what was originally a gothic arch design fashioned with mouldings on the wall.

A typical three-sided gallery with decorative mouldings, graces the interior. The mouldings and the original pews, all recently grained, gleam like highly polished wood, generating a righ, warm atmosphere. An ornately carved pulpit, the successor to the old "bull pulpit" which was only accessible by ladder, is in keeping with its antique surroundings.

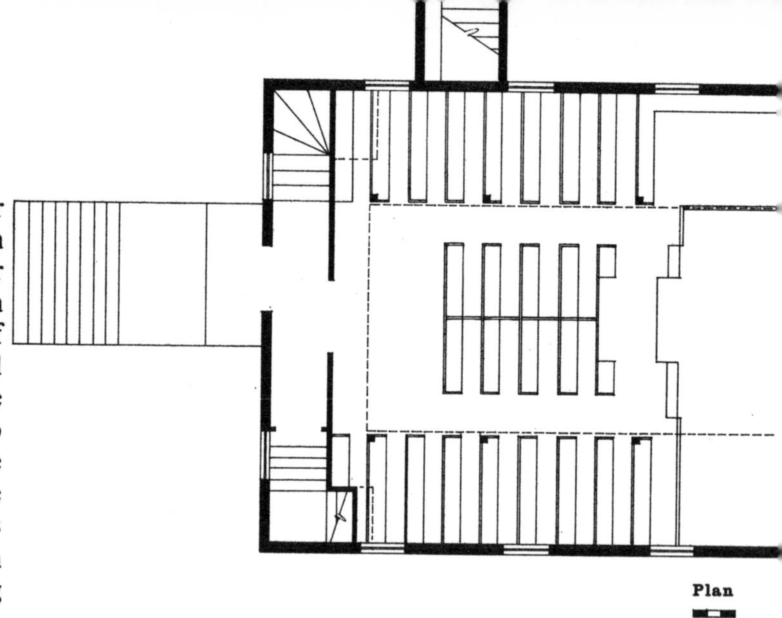

Plan

In fact, very few changes have been made over the years, and none have been unsympathetic. An electric organ has been added, the tuning fork and pitch pipe having long since disappeared. In 1941, on the occasion of the 132nd anniversary, the oil lamps were lit as usual and the service began; then, a dramatic moment came when the lamps were symbolically lowered and new electric light suddenly flooded the room. Ironically now, due to a new awareness of the church's heritage, the old wooden candelabras and brass, alladin lamps have been re-installed. Special evensong services are held by the light of candles and kerosene.

A number of telling relics are still extant and available for visitors to see. A shiny brass spittoon is strategically placed near the pulpit as in days gone by. Also on display, is the original, glass communion set. Other cherished items include an antique, long-handled collection bag and an aged copy of the New Testament printed in German, once owned by a former parishioner.

Throughout the 170-year history, the congregation has gained a reputation for innovations and courageous endeavours. For example, the first two people to be baptized by immersion in Canada were said to have been members of this church. A most spirited event happened in June of 1828, when six ladies of the North West Range congregation walked 40 miles to Wolfville to cast their vote in favour of the founding of Horton Academy, which later became Acadia University. And not only did the determined ladies walk the distance, but they did so barefoot in order to preserve their shoes for the auspicious occasion.

It is not surprising that the congregation, many of whom are descendants of the original French and German settlers, can still accomplish much through perseverance. About ten years ago, it was felt that a basement, to serve as a church hall, would be an asset. Instead of hiring a contractor to jack up the structure and build a foundation, a much more difficult and less costly approach was taken. A large-scale volunteer effort was organized; the men of the community and surrounding area, approximately 25 in number, contributed two nights a week free labour, until a ten-foot basement was excavated, by hand, underneath the church. The digging required long hours of arduous work, and took two years to complete. The result is ideal; the spacious modern hall not only provides a new facility but does not detract in the least from the appearance of the historic meeting house.

St.Mary's Basilica, Halifax

St. Mary's Basilica stands not only as the leading house of worship of the Roman Catholic Archdiocese of Halifax, but also as a tangible reminder of the religious freedom that was finally achieved after years of intolerance and hardship.

English penal laws were in effect in Nova Scotia from 1713, but it was not until after the expulsion, in 1755, of the Acadians, who had refused to swear the oath of allegiance to the King on religious grounds, that religious and other freedoms were seriously curtailed for Roman Catholics. In 1758, a law was passed in Nova Scotia excluding Roman Catholics from the House of Representatives and from owning land. A further act "for the establishment of religious worship in the Province, and for suppressing Popery" was passed; this act decreed the establishment of the Church of England, and granted full liberty of conscience and rights of public worship to all dissenting protestants, but not to papists. "Popish priests" were required to leave the province "on or before 25th of March, 1759", and any person that harboured a popish priest would be fined £50 and would be "set in a pillory".

However, the English authorities in Halifax were mortally afraid of the Micmac Indians and knew that only Abbé Antoine Maillard, the French catholic missionary priest had any influence over them. So Maillard was appointed an official missionary to the Indians and to the Acadians who were returning. Abbé Maillard came to Halifax about 1760, and celebrated the first mass in a barn which was situated approximately where the corner of Tobin and Barrington streets is today.

By 1781, three years after the Catholic Relief Act had been passed in England, the flames of intolerance were beginning to die down. Five Irish catholics in Halifax petitioned the Governor of Nova Scotia for the repeal of two statutes of the penal laws. Finally, on July 2, 1784, the king ratified the bill of religious freedom so that the Nova Scotia catholics could acquire land and build churches for public worship. Just seventeen days later, the frame of the first catholic church was raised on the lot of land bordered by Grafton and Barrington streets and Spring Garden Road. The small, wooden church, known at St. Peter's, served the parish for about 45 years; later, it was dismantled and sent across the harbour, along with its name, to become the first catholic church in Dartmouth.

In 1801, Father Edmund Burke, one of the most renowned figures of early church life in Canada, came to Halifax. Edmund Burke was a scholar, wit and humanitarian who had spent the previous seven years as Ontario's first English-speaking missionary, living in the wilds with the Indians. In 1818, he was consecrated the first Vicar Apostolic or Bishop of Nova Scotia. Bishop Burke took a great interest in engineering, as well as literary and religious pursuits, so it is not surprising to find that he had a hand in drawing up plans for a new cathedral. In June of 1820, he wrote to the Archbishop of Dublin: "We have just begun to build a cathedral here which will cost us at least ten thousand pounds sterling. The extreme length of the church is 106 feet and the breadth 66 feet, the walls lime and stone, cut stone in the whole front." And by that time, the new church was needed as there were approximately 2000 catholics in Halifax.

Unfortunately, Bishop Burke did not live long enough to see the completion of his magnificent, stone cathedral. First named St. Peter's after its predecessor, the cathedral opened for service in 1829; four years later, the name was changed to St. Mary's Cathedral. It was a fine edifice, constructed of native ironstone with sandstone trim, and had a square tower topped with four finials. Along each side, there were two tiers of seven windows, an upper tier of plain gothic arched windows and a lower tier of square windows. The sober and dignified front façade was punctuated by three entrances of gothic arch design and above these, three unembellished windows, also in the shape of gothic arches. A further three gothic windows, one above the other, ornamented the central tower. Inside, there was a superb, vaulted ceiling held aloft by a row of pillars on each side of the nave. There were two side galleries, and beneath them, closed box pews.

St. Mary's Cathedral underwent extensive changes during Archbishop Thomas Connolly's episcopate. In 1863, the building was lengthened to 190 feet to accommodate a chancel and large organ. As well, the double tiers of windows on each side of the church were converted to a single tier of long, gothic windows. Inside, the galleries were removed altogether, and the old box pews were replaced with a more up-to-date variety. The vaulted ceiling which had been almost unadorned was now heavily embellished in the Victorian gothic style.

The most startling and visible change, however, was the addition of the highly ornate Victorian façade which was designed by architect Patrick Charles Keely of New York. Keely had designed approximately 500 churches in North America. Thus, in 1863, the old, square tower was taken down; in 1868 Archbishop Connolly wrote to the Foreign Office in London requesting permission to quarry seven or eight hundred tons of granite from the government's property on the shores of the North West Arm. "There is enough stone in that quarry to build all the fortifications of the British Empire and after to build as many cities as large as London," he argued eloquently. Permission was granted and the new, monumental façade was constructed including, what is reputed to be, the highest, dressed granite spire in North America. Finally, on September 7, 1874, the cross was placed atop the spire, exactly 189 feet above the sidewalk.

Other more minor changes have taken place over the years. The church was first heated by stoves which were replaced, in 1859, by a hot air furnace which was, in turn, replaced by an oil furnace in 1959. Oil lamps were used until 1897, when electricity and gas gleamed from the brackets on the pillars. In

1953, the present indirect lighting system was installed, and the brackets removed. Also, in this century, the sanctuaries were enlarged, and a further extension at the back of the church added storage and office space.

A number of notable people have been connected with the church, including Sir John S. D. Thompson, the fourth Prime Minister of Canada, who was buried from St. Mary's on January 3, 1895. And the front pew on the west side of the central aisle is always reserved for the Lieutenant-Governor of Nova Scotia.

In 1950, the title of Basilica was bestowed on St. Mary's by Pope Pius XII. Today, St. Mary's co-exists at its busy location not only with neighbouring United and Presbyterian churches, but also with modern office towers and the rush of downtown traffic. The eleven-bell chimes ring out high above the hurrying throngs, offering an invitation to worship.

William Black Memorial, Glen Margaret

This small, frame church is located in Glen Margaret, a community about 16 miles southwest of Halifax, on the eastern shore of St. Margaret's Bay. The church was named in honour of the founder of Methodism in Canada.

William Black, or "Bishop Black" as he was known, was born in 1760, the son of a Scottish father and Yorkshire mother. The Black family settled in Amherst, Nova Scotia, as part of a migration of Yorkshiremen to Cumberland County between 1770 and 1775. These settlers came to Nova Scotia on the instigation of Governor Franklyn who considered them to be cultured, hardy, thrifty, and above all, loyal to Britain.

An account in *The Halifax Herald* on June 27, 1896, states that William Black was "converted at the age of 19" and shortly thereafter he left home to preach throughout Nova Scotia, New Brunswick, and Prince Edward Island. He also travelled to the United States and preached the first Methodist sermon in Boston.

The mode of travel for clergymen in these early days was mostly by foot. It was not unusual for ministers to walk great distances to serve their congregations. The hardships of travel were exhausting, and many ministers perished as they moved from place to place. For example, in the winter of 1795, one minister froze to death while attempting to walk the 30 miles from Chester to Windsor. William Black, himself, once walked 130 miles from Shelburne to Windsor to preach there.

Glen Margaret was originally known as the "Lower Ward"; fishing, farming, lumbering, and trade with the West Indies were the main means of livelihood. The first Methodist services in Glen Margaret were held in the home of Alexander Renfrew in the 1780's. The William Black Memorial Church was built in 1821, by volunteer labour, and was first called "The Meeting House". Typically, it resembled a traditional church building in plan, with the pulpit and main entrance opposite each other on the long axis.

In 1834, the church was named "Wesleyan-Methodist Church", and sometime thereafter, it was said to have been visited by

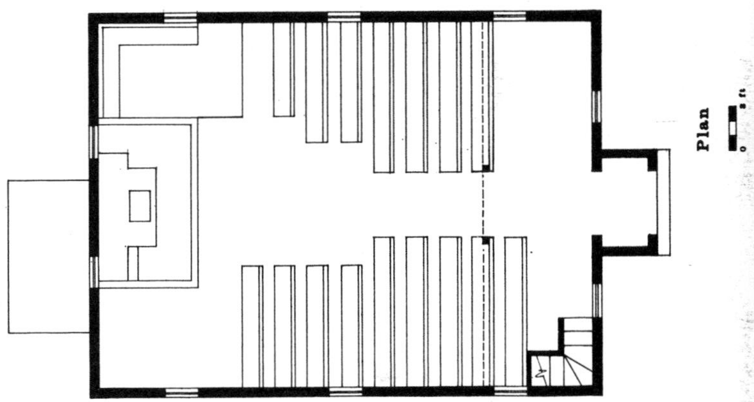

Plan

William Black. By 1884, the building had deteriorated to such a degree that plans were made to sell the property, with the proceeds to be used to refurnish a neighbouring parsonage. However, the church was not sold, and was subsequently repaired and refurbished in 1895. In 1925, with the union of Methodists, Congregationalists and Presbyterians, the United Church of Canada assumed ownership of the property. In 1939, the church was given its present name.

The architecture of William Black Memorial is austere, reminiscent of the New England vernacular style with its simple, box-like form. It is devoid of ornamentation or embellishment except for light moulding at the roofline and return at the corners. The straight-line profile is eased somewhat by the gentle curve of the window heads. Regardless of its formal appearance, the building has a pleasant scale by virtue of its small size. Also, the church is enhanced by its rural setting. A low fence encloses the property, and the side and rear yards serve as a cemetery. A small lake behind the church completes the peaceful setting. The tower was added in 1953, built by a local resident in memory of his parents.

However plain the exterior, the number of windows make the interior airy and bright, and the wood-planked floor and dark-stained pews add warmth. The ceiling forms a simple arch, and a small balcony is located over the entry. One cherished piece of furniture is an ebony baptismal font, originally brought over from Scotland, and believed to be at least 200 years old.

Should you visit the church on a Sunday morning in the summer, the quiet of the day will be broken only by the ringing of the church bell, and you will be greeted by a friendly congregation, proud of their heritage and the legacy of William Black.

Cole Harbour Meeting House

At the top of Long Hill, in the rural farmland just outside the city of Dartmouth, overlooking the Cole Harbour Salt Marsh and the beaches of the Eastern Shore, sits a small, church-like building. Set back from the edge of the hill, and surrounded on two sides by trees which have grown up in the area of the old cemetery, the Cole Harbour Meeting House may be passed by almost unnoticed.

The sign over the door proclaims the meeting house to have been constructed in 1823, but many of the older residents believe the existing building was constructed two or three years later on the foundations of the 1823 building.

Historical and archeological research has produced solid evidence of a building existing and services being held in 1823; the later history is somewhat vague as befits any rural farming community. There was never a conscious effort to document the history of the meeting house, as it was treated as always having stood there and having been used by the community. That life went on in this normal fashion is borne out by the notation in the 1827 *Minute Book of the Methodist Church of Nova Scotia District*. Cole Harbour is listed as having a chapel of the size approximately 16 feet by 20 feet with no pews and a small debt, the emphasis being on the small debt.

Later research, from a series of articles in the *Dartmouth Partiot* of 1910-1911, yields a reference to one Edward Stevens who "...put up the frame of the Meeting House at Cole Harbour about 85 years ago". That would support evidence that the date of the existing meeting house is 1825. This site is marked and noted "Wesleyan Chapel" on the 1852 chart compiled for the Royal Navy by Captain Bayfield.

The meeting house is a plain building, simple in line and form, covered by a pitched roof, and entered into through a small vestibule at the west end. Only the vestibule has any decoration, a simple moulding and return. The door is an enlarged gothic arch. The entry is flanked on the main gable wall by a gothic window on each side, while in the apex of the gable is a circular window.

The north and south elevations, which are the long sides of the building, are pierced by two gothic windows which provide the main light to the interior. There is no stained glass, no decoration, just the simple, shelter allowing for no visual distraction from the business at hand, whether sacred or secular. On the east side, a lean-to addition of the late 1970's provides washroom facilities, a sign of the continuing use of this meeting house in the present day.

A visual inspection of the interior gives clues to changes made at various times. The September 24, 1880, issue of the *Wesleyan* gives details of a picnic which raised the sum of $70.00, quite sufficient to make proposed repairs. These repairs were probably the result of the creation of a separate Anglican parish for Cole Harbour, including Eastern Passage and Cow Bay, in 1871, leaving the all-denomination meeting house as the Methodist church for the area. On the floor of the meeting house are traces of columns which supported a small gallery at the west end of the building. An iron tie rod was put in place to help stabilize the walls and balance uneven roof thrust when the walls began to settle. The exact date of these renovations is not known, but there is record of renovation in 1892. A concrete foundation has been placed under the building creating a crawl space, access to which is by a panel on the south elevation.

The interior, like the exterior, is plain and simple space although the ceiling is cone-vaulted. The original plaster on lath can be found on all the walls and the ceiling, when one looks under the existing finishes of painted fibreboard on the walls and perforated acoustic tile on the ceiling.

In 1961, the meeting house ceased to function as the United Church in the area, as the congregation moved to the Bisset Road United Church. The building was then rented out for commercial use as an army-navy surplus clothing store, run by Mr. DeWolfe who kept the meeting house heated and protected from abandonment and vandalism.

By 1973, the Cole Harbour Rural Heritage Society was well established, and was granted permission to use and restore the building. Further help came from a grant of $2,000 in 1975, under the "Little Red Schoolhouse" program. Now the meeting house once again fulfills the purpose for which it was originally constructed: as a church for ecumenical services; as an exhibition centre; as a public meeting house for the various societies, including senior citizens and the Rural Heritage Society.

The meeting house is painted white with a shingled roof, and stands out in contrast to the current visual impact of the rapidly expanding suburbs built by the Nova Scotia Housing Commission in the vinyl siding aesthetic.

The mill stones which stand to the south of the meeting house are the only remaining parts of Cole Harbour's first oat mill, built in the 1830's by James Bissett, an active participant in the affairs of the community. They stand as if to protect the meeeting house from the onslaught of the proposed four-lane highway, the last element in transforming Cole Harbour into another Dartmouth suburb. However, the Rural Heritage Society is hopeful that the meeting house will continue to serve the community for at least another 150 years.

St. Patrick's,
Sydney

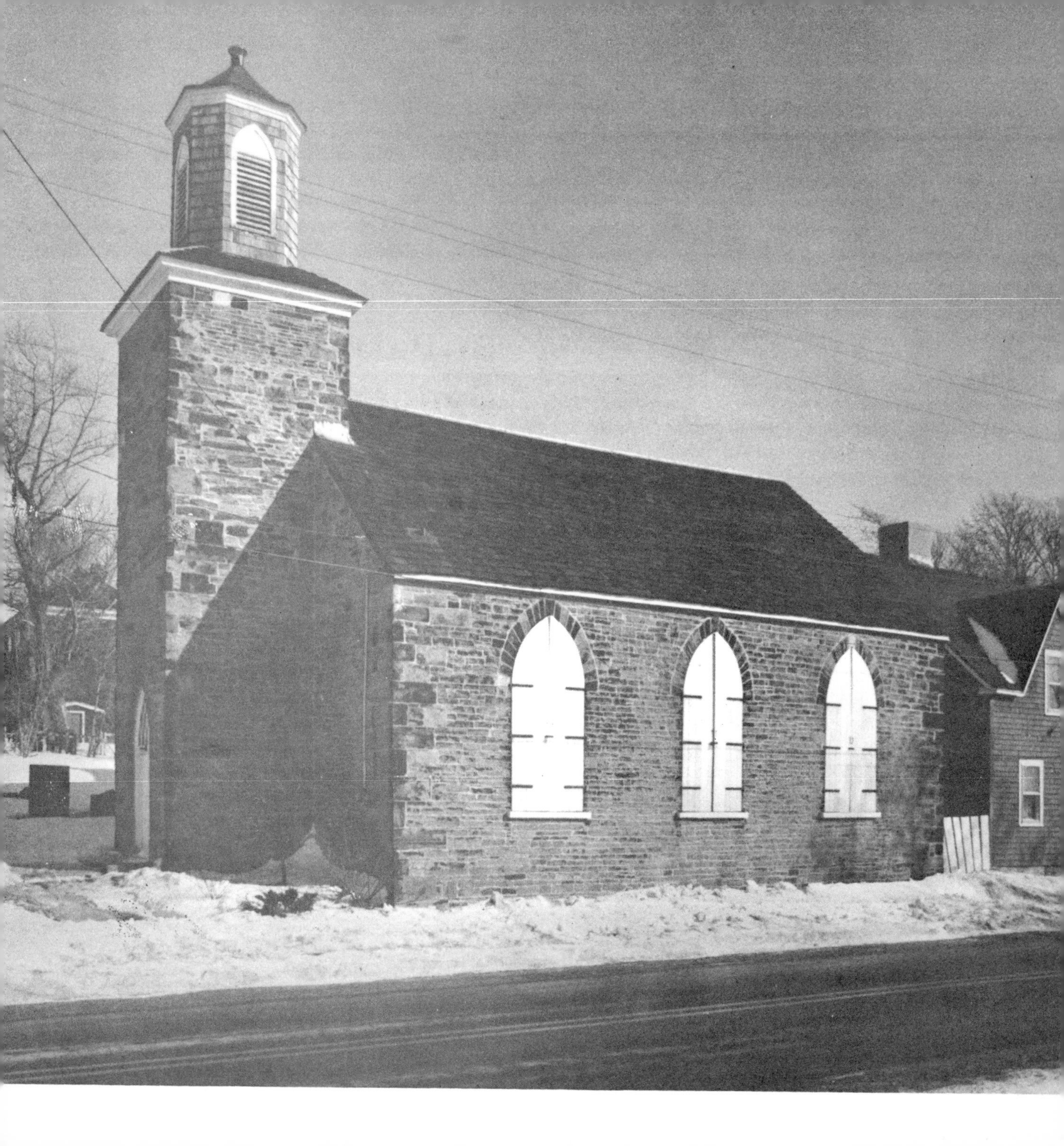

Within thirty years after the town of Sydney had been laid out, the Roman catholics had erected a small, wooden chapel on the Esplanade, just a few blocks from St. George's Anglican Church. The chapel was built on land owned by John Wilson, a local merchant, militia captain and founder of Sydney. In 1823, at the age of 74 years, Wilson died, and his widow gave the land and chapel to Rev. Henry McKeagney.

McKeagney was the first permanent catholic priest in Sydney, having been officially appointed in 1825. By 1828, his parishioners had collected enough money to commence the building of a stone church on Wilson's land in the same location as the wooden chapel. Completed about 1830, the new church was first called St. Peter's. The adjoining graveyard was originally called St. Henry's, but by 1853, both the church and the graveyard were known by the present name of St. Patrick's.

The new church was sturdily constructed in stone with walls three feet thick. For the most part, the stone was quarried in the vicinity and brought to the site on barges. However, some stone also came from the ruins of the great French fortress at Louisbourg, 22 miles away. In anticipation of the architecture of the church, Judge T.C. Haliburton observed in 1829, "The Roman Catholics have laid the foundations of a spacious stone chapel which, if completed according to the design, will be a great ornament to Sydney." And much later, in 1864, Rev. R.J. Uniacke, Rector of St. George's Anglican Church, stated, "The Roman Catholics have a neat chapel....built of stone in the gothic style with tower and cupola situated near the water upon the Esplanade."

The church, indeed, must have added to the attractiveness of the community in the early days, just as its rustic character adds to the city of Sydney today. Its stone construction, small scale, and particular style of primitive gothic architecture, are reminiscent of many an English country church. One interesting and unusual feature of the church is the side chancel. Originally, the parishioners sat at right angles to the main entrance facing the chancel; their backs would have been to the windows along the Esplanade, allowing a good deal of light to come in over their shoulders. In the mid-19th century, however, this configuration was changed; the side chancel became the vestry and the altar was moved to the front of the nave. At the same time too, balconies were added around three sides of the nave.

On top of the square stone tower, there is an octagonal lantern with round-headed openings and a conical roof cap. Originally the cupola was sheathed in metal and more rounded in shape, with a domed roof cap surmounted by a cross.

St. Patrick's was used until 1874, when the Sacred Heart Church on George Street was built, and the congregation from St. Patrick's moved there. But in 1876, the Sacred Heart

Church burned down, and St. Patrick's was once again occupied. This was temporary, however, until the new Sacred Heart Church was re-built in 1889. Then the use of St. Patrick's was discontinued for a time.

About 1900, the church was taken over as a place of worship by the Lebanese families when they first started coming to Sydney. The Lebanese were part of the great influx of immigrants who came to Sydney between the turn of the century and the end of World War I. During those years, Sydney became a boom town, increasing its population rapidly from about 2,500 inhabitants to 25,000 inhabitants. Unlike the Polish, Lithuanian and other European immigrants who came to work in the steel plant, the Lebanese came as merchants to serve the needs of the growing population. Father Saoib, who had been specially brought out from Lebanon, ministered his flock at St. Patrick's until he died about 1950.

When the Lebanese congregation dispersed, the Ancient Order of Hibernians, a temperance group, used the church as a meeting hall until about 1960, when they disbanded and left the building vacant. In 1966, the Old Sydney Historical Society took possession of St. Patrick's for use as a museum. Firstly, the Society replaced the deteriorating floorboards and reconstructed the old balconies. Since most of the plaster had fallen from ceiling and walls, the Society decided that the bare stone walls and exposed, pegged ceiling beams would be adequate, and even appropriate, for the new use of the building as a museum. Outside shutters were added to prevent broken windows and vandalism during the winter months when the museum is closed.

Today the museum portrays the history of Sydney and Cape Breton through photographs and interesting artifacts including the Old Sydney Whipping Post, part of the Transatlantic cable, and Gaelic bibles brought to Sydney by Scottish settlers at about the time St. Patrick's was built. Thus, St. Patrick's, the oldest Roman catholic church in Cape Breton, has a new and fitting message to deliver — the preservation of Sydney's unique heritage.

St. John's, Sackville

St. John's Anglican, the mother church of the parish of Sackville, was built in 1829, and stands on top of a hill, a visible landmark from the approaches to Sackville on the old Windsor road. Sackville is a modern-day suburb about 14 miles west of Halifax; it had its beginnings as a separate district, protected by its own fort, as early as 1749. It became a separate parish by the establishment of boundaries in 1804.

Questions arise as to the earliest church on the site and, also, as to the number of churches previously built there. The earliest was either in 1790 or 1805, with a subsequent church being constructed in 1807 and not being finished until 1812. The current church was constructed after a fire destroyed the previous one on November 10, 1828 in the sight of those parishioners gathered for divine worship.

On the 24th of that month, plans were made for the building of a new St. John's, and £40 was subscribed, a woefully inadequate sum but a sign of good faith. The parish persevered, and on November 28, 1830, the current church was consecrated by Rt. Rev. John Ingles, Bishop of Nova Scotia. The construction is attributed to only three men, certainly skilled carpenters, whose work held fast until 1959, when the tower and spire were restored.

St. John's is a Georgian church, and one immediately recognizes the similarity to St. Paul's in Halifax or the Church of Saint John at Cornwallis. The massing of the church is visually uncluttered with a simple rectangular plan and pitched roof. The vestibule and chancel are smaller versions of the nave, giving visual unity to the line and mass of the church. The fine, classical steeple has a square tower surmounted by an octagonal belfry and a tall, slim spire. While the proportions and detailing of St. John's are classical, most of the windows have gothic arches.

There had been a dispute in the parish in 1828, as to whether a church should be re-built. A letter in the *Acadian Recorder* on December 15, 1828, seriously presents the argument that, as the parish had no resident clergyman, perhaps money from the Society for the Propagation of the Gospel was warranted. A demand for getting a minister appears to have had much support. The first resident rector of this church was the Rev. Archibald Gray who stayed for nineteen years. Gray began to acquire for the church the ornaments necessary to service. A chalice and paten were purchased for £19, and several items such as prayer books and plates were acquired. In 1843, Mr. Gray asked the parishioners to make up for the lack of money, provided by the Society, which had been withdrawn by the English Parliament. A bond was issued for Rev. Gray's support, as long as each subscriber remained a resident in the parish.

Mr. Gray's years were good ones for St. John's. In 1844, extra pews were placed in the gallery to accommodate members, the numbers of which had increased. The departure of Rev. Gray from the parish in 1852, inaugurated a period of difficulty for the parish. Ministers did not stay long, the shortest stay being three months. The Rev. Mr. T.H. Drumm stayed one year, leaving because the parish failed to provide a rectory, and he argued that his salary of £75 was inadequate to provide for a family and pay rent. The Rev. W.G. Gray, son of Rev. Archibald Gray, and the Rev. E. Gilpin, lasted only three months as did the teacher-minister Rev. Mulholland. In 1859, the Rev. W.R. Cochran was appointed to the parish, and fortunately for St. John's, he stayed until 1863. Considerable progress under his direction was made, the most important being the purchase of land for a rectory.

A variety of others served the parish but in 1876, the Rev. William Ellis became rector, and the parish benefitted greatly. Mr. Ellis was a strong character and despite physical handicap, worked his 16 years in the parish without faltering. He demanded from his parishioners much; the men were to remove hats in the cemetery even on the coldest days; the method of burial services was to meet his approval, and Sunday services were to be precedent to all things. On the other hand, Mr. Ellis was compassionate and showed great kindness to his parish.

In 1888, Rev. Ellis began a movement to restore the church. In 1891, the chancel was added and the box pews and three-decker pulpit were removed. The doors of the box pews now form panelling around the chancel. The centre window in the east end of the church, depicting the Last Supper, is in memory of Mr. Ellis who died in 1900 and lies buried in St. John's churchyard.

The years immediately after Mr. Ellis's service were marked once again by little progress, the parish being served by ministers who stayed only long enough to be recorded by pen, not deeds. During the first half on the 20th century, Sackville grew from being a country village to a fringe community on the edge of the ever-growing Halifax-Dartmouth metropolis. By the 1940's, it was considered a suburban parish. All of this development took place during the rectorship of Rev. A. Tyers who served from 1919 until 1946, the longest service seen in St. John's parish. Mr. Tyers walked much especially if conditions were such that an automobile could not carry him. During his time, the second rectory was built, being completed in 1934. Mr. Tyers died in 1957, and like Rev. Ellis, he too, lies buried in St. John's churchyard.

From 1945 until the present, the parish has been self-supporting. A concrete foundation was put under the church and that space, which is used for a meeting room, is served by a narrow staircase from the outside.

A look at the photos from 1890 shows the church in a more original state, with decoration in the form of applied pilasters, cornice returns, and narrow clapboards. However, the church still maintains its historic form and graceful steeple, and remains a most visible landmark.

CONCLUSION

Let us consider the future of Nova Scotia's oldest churches.

Because of the changing settlement patterns, congregations are often smaller. The diminished church populations must, in some cases, bear the burden of upkeep for more than one church. For example, there is the Annapolis parish that maintains, and worships in, three historic churches — St. Luke's in Annapolis Royal, Christ Church in Karsdale and All Saints' in Granville Centre.

This situation may, at first glance, sound ominous for the continued existence of the churches. But there are other important factors. Firstly, the congregations, however small, take good care of their churches, and appreciate the historic value of the buildings. It is a joy, for instance, to visit Old St. Edward's on a summer day and to be greeted by two friendly parishioners who proudly point out the historic and architectural merits of their church.

Secondly, and perhaps most importantly, there is a growing awareness of our heritage and our past. This thirst for knowledge and experience of our past is felt on a national level as we try to search for a national identity. Also, it is the wish of the different provinces and areas in Canada to establish a regional identity.

In Nova Scotia, unlike other regions, we are fortunate to have strong evidence of the past. Nova Scotia's identity, like the sea, is all around us. And the most visible, tangible, and understandable part of our heritage and our identity is our buildings.

These 22 churches from the earliest building period contribute significantly to our distinctive identity. Thus, Nova Scotia's most historic churches must be carefully guarded, kept in trust for future Nova Scotians and Canadians. The churches remain a steadfast constant in our world of change.

BIBLIOGRAPHY & CREDITS

Introduction

MacKinnon, I. F., *Settlements and Churches in Nova Scotia 1749-1776,* Walker Press, (1930).

Saunders, E. M., *History of the Baptists in the Maritime Provinces,* Press of John Burgoyne, 1902.

Eaton, A. W. H., *The Church in Nova Scotia, and the Tory Clergy of the Revolution*, T. Whittaker, 1891.

Vernon, C.W., *Bicentenary Sketches and Early Days of the Church in Nova Scotia*, The Chronicle Printing Company, 1910.

Bourinot, Sir John G., *Builders of Nova Scotia*, Copp-Clark Company, 1900.

Johnston, A. A., *A History of the Catholic Church in Eastern Nova Scotia*, Vol. I, 1611-1827, St. Francis Xavier University Press, 1960.

Coverstone, Jean L., *Church Architecture in Nova Scotia from 1750-1867,* a thesis submitted to the University of Notre Dame, Indiana, 1972.

Smith, Rev. T. Watson, "The Romance of Early Methodism in Nova Scotia", The Halifax Herald, June 27, 1896.

Levy, G. E., *The Baptists of the Maritime Provinces 1753-1946,* Barnes-Hopkins Ltd., 1946.

Design Influences

Sinnott, E. W., *Meeting House and Church in Early New England*, McGraw-Hill Book Company Inc., 1963.

Gowans, Alan, "New England Architecture in Nova Scotia", The Art Quarterly, Spring 1962.

Rose, Harold, *Colonial Houses of Worship in America*, Hastings House, 1963-64.

Gibbs, James, *The Rules for Drawing the Several Parts of Architecture*, Hodder & Stoughton Limited, 1947.

Benjamin, Asher, *The American Builder's Companion*, reprinted by General Publishing Company, 1969.

Palladio, Andrea, *The Four Books of Architecture*, reprinted by General Publishing Company, 1965.

Early Construction

Peterson, Charles E., editor, *Building Early America*, Clitton Press, 1976.

Rempel, John, *Building With Wood*, University of Toronto Press, 1980.

Cummings, A.L., *Architecture in Early New England*, Meriden Gravure Company, 1967.

Patterson, Rev. George, *A History of the County of Pictou, Nova Scotia*, facsimile edition, Mika Studio, 1972.

Sloan, Eric, *A Museum of Early American Tools*, Ballantine Books, 1974.

Preserving Historic Structures in Canada: Wood, a draft manual, Restoration Services Division, Parks Canada, 1978.

Churches

Akins, T. B., *History of Halifax City*, facsimile edition, Mika Publishing, 1973.

Raddall, Thomas H., *Halifax Warden of the North*, McClelland and Stewart Ltd., 1971.

Founded Upon a Rock, Heritage Trust of Nova Scotia, 1967.

St. Paul's Church, Halifax, N.S., a booklet published by St. Paul's Church.

Harris, R. V., *The Church of St. Paul in Halifax, Nova Scotia: 1749-1949*, Ryerson, 1949.

Gibson, M. Allen, "St. Paul's Church of England, Halifax", The Chronicle-Herald, July 6, 1955.

Thomas, C. E., "Tutty, William", *Dictionary of Canadian Biography*, Vol. III, pp. 634, 635, University of Toronto Press, 1974.

Read, F. C., "An Historical Sketch, St. John's Anglican Church", St. John's Church, 1971.

Gibson, M. Allen, "St. John's Church of England, Lunenburg", The Chronicle-Herald, November 4, 1954.

Fingard, Judith, "Moreau, Jean-Baptiste", *Dictionary of Canadian Biography*, Vol. III, p. 473, University of Toronto Press, 1974.

DesBrisay, Mather B., "The Historical Church of Lunenburg", The Halifax Herald, July 11, 1896.

DesBrisay, M. B., *History of the County of Lunenburg*, facsimile edition, Mika Studio, 1972.

Thomas, C. E., "Breynton, John", *Dictionary of Canadian Biography*, Vol. IV, pp. 93, 94, University of Toronto Press, 1979.

Harris, R. V., Rev. H. G. Hodder, *A Brief History of St. George's Church*, St. George's Church, 1975.

Nickerson, Alex, "Lutherans founded the Little Dutch Church", The Mail Star, September 28, 1981.

Doane, Frank A., "The Old Meeting House: 1765, Barrington, N.S.", The United Churchman, June 28, 1933.

Gibson, M. Allen, "Old Meeting House, The United Church of Canada, Barrington", The Chronicle-Herald, March 27, 1954.

Richardson, Evelyn M., *Barrington's Old Meeting House*, reprinted from Advertiser Blossom edition, Kentville Advertiser, May, 1968.

"Service Marks 200th Anniversary of Barrington's Old Meeting House", The Chronicle-Herald, September 15, 1965.

Legge, J. H., *St. George's Sydney, A Layman's Study*, a booklet published by St. George's, 1971.

Smith, Venerable Archdeacon, "The Historic Anglican Church at Sydney", The Halifax Herald, June 27, 1896.

Gibson, M. Allen, "St. George's Church of England, Sydney", The Chronicle-Herald, June 20, 1953.

Gibson, M. Allen, "To Preserve Historic St. Edward's Church", The Diocesan Times, July 1956.

Macdonald, S. E. G., *Old St. Edward's Church, Clementsport, N.S.*, an unpublished and undated manuscript.

"Old St. Edward's Church, The Parish of Clements, The Anglican Church of Canada, Clementsport, Nova Scotia", a pamphlet published by St. Edward's.

Sharp, Donald D. M., "Old Holy Trinity Church", a pamphlet published by Holy Trinity Church, 1977.

Inglis, Rev. Dr. Charles, "Letter to Dr. Morice", September 3, 1796.

Inglis, Rev. Dr. Charles, "Letter to Rev. Wiswall", August 14, 1796.

"Old Holy Trinity Church (Middleton) to be Restored", The Diocesan Times, August 1951.

Gibson, M. Allen, "Old Holy Trinity Anglican Church, Middleton", The Chronicle-Herald, April 13, 1960.

Home, Pauline, Margaret Martin, Bessie Murray and K. B. Wainwright, *St. Mary's Church, Auburn, N.S. 1790*, Heritage Trust of Nova Scotia, 1967.

"Touch up historic church", The Chronicle-Herald, October 9, 1970.

Clattenburg, M. D., "Early Days in Avon Deanery", The Diocesan Times, April 1960.

Inglis, Rev. Dr. Charles, "Letter to Dr. Morice", October 16, 1789.

Inglis, Rev. Dr. Charles, *Journal of Occurances 1785-1810*, entries for September 22, 1790, September 25, 1790, September 30, 1790, October 4, 1790, October 10, 1790, an unpublished manuscript.

Gibson, M. Allen, "Christ Church Anglican, Karsdale", The Chronicle-Herald, December 29, 1956.

Findlay, E. M., "The Presbyterian Covenanter Church of Grand Pré", a manuscript, May 26, 1972.

Kirkconnell, Watson, editor, *The Diary of Deacon Elihu Woodworth*, Wolfville Historical Society, 1972.

Historical Sketch of Church of St. John, a booklet published by St. John's Church, 1911, 1960, 1980.

Gibson, M. Allen, "St. John's Anglican Church, Church Street", The Chronicle-Herald, August 8, 1959.

"St. John's Church, Cornwallis", The Diocesan Times, February 1947.

Potter, Rae, Johanna Holland, Deacon Ken Robinson, "A Brief Historical Portrait of the Life & Ministry of the Goat Island Baptist Church, Upper Clements, N. S.", a pamphlet published by Deep Brook United Baptist Pastorate.

Gibson, M. Allen, "All Saints Anglican Church, Granville Centre", The Chronicle-Herald, November 24, 1964.

Perkins, Charlotte, *Historic Paper of St. Luke's Church*, 1922.

Perkins, Charlotte, *The Romance of Old Annapolis Royal*, pp. 54-59, revised edition, Historical Association of Annapolis Royal, 1952.

Gibson, M. Allen, "St. Luke's Church of England, Annapolis Royal", The Chronicle-Herald, July 11, 1953.

How, Rev. Henry, "St. Luke's, Annapolis Royal, Graphic and Interesting Account of a Service held Seventy-five Years Ago", The Annapolis Spectator, December 23, 1908.

Owen, Mrs. Farish, "Notes on St. Luke's Church", a manuscript, September 1974.

"Parish of St. Luke's Annapolis Royal, N.S., Brief Historical Sketch", est. 1970.

Savary, A. W., "French and Anglican Churches at Annapolis Royal", The Annapolis Spectator, August 24, 1910.

Bayer, C. Walter, *Christ Church, Dartmouth, Nova Scotia 1817-1959*, a book published by Christ Church, 1960.

Vernon, C. W., *The Story of Christ Church Dartmouth*, Weeks Printing Company,1917.

Gibson, M. Allen, "United Baptist Church, North West", The Chronicle-Herald, November 7, 1959.

"157 Anniversary, Church to Celebrate With Special Service", The Chronicle-Herald, October 31, 1966.

Records of the Baptist Church, North West Range, Lunenburg County, Nova Scotia, see entry of November 3, 1809.

Levy, G. E., *The Baptists of the Maritime Provinces*, pp. 1-3, and pp. 54, 55, 64, 65, Barnes-Hopkins Ltd., 1946.

Levy, George E., *The Diary of Joseph Dimock*, Lancelot Press, 1979.

Burns, Evelyn, "Saint Mary's Basilica, A Short History and Guide", a pamphlet published by St. Mary's Basilica, June 15, 1972.

Hinds, Barbara, "Basilica's Cornerstone was laid 151 years ago", The Mail-Star, 1971.

Gibson, M. Allen, "St. Mary's Basilica Halifax", The Chronicle-Herald, June 23, 1956.

Foley, Rev. William, *The Centenary of St. Mary's Cathedral, Halifax, N.S. 1820-1920*, a book published by St. Mary's Cathedral, 1920.

Alfred, Rev. Brother, "The Right Rev. Edmund Burke, D.D., 'Apostle of Upper Canada', Bishop of Zion, First Vicar Apostolic of Nova Scotia: 1753-1820", from *The Canadian Catholic Historical Association Report*, 1942.

William Black Memorial Church, 150th Anniversary — 1971, a booklet published by William Black Memorial Church, 1971.

Morgan, Robert J., "Brief History of St. Patrick's Church, Situated on the Esplanade, Sydney, N.S.", a manuscript.

Tufts, Rev. Karl H., *A Short History of the Parish of Sackville, N.S. 1790-1960*, a booklet published by St. John's Sackville, 1960.

Davis, Rev. B. J., "St. John's Church", The Diocesan Times, November 1952.

CREDITS

Drawings and illustrations were prepared by staff in the offices of MacFawn and Rogers Architects, and Architectural Resource Consultants Limited. The Hollis Street elevation of Province House, Halifax was done by A. W. Wallace.

Editor — Elizabeth A. Pacey

Graphics and Layout — G. Edward MacFarlane

Photography

Early Construction

detail of a ship's knee	John Lavers
detail of wooden pegged post and beam	John Lavers
St. Mary's, Auburn	John Lavers

Churches

1.	St. Paul's, Halifax	Arthur Carter
	St. Paul's, interior	John Lavers
	St. Paul's, steeple detail	John Lavers
	St. Paul's, circa 1759	from an engraving by Richard Short, from the Public Archives of Nova Scotia collection
	St. Paul's, east elevation	Nova Scotia Information Service, 1979
	brick nogging	John Lavers
2.	St. John's, Lunenburg	Allan Duffus

3.	Little Dutch Church	John Lavers
	Little Dutch Church, interior	from the Public Archives of Nova Scotia collection
	Little Dutch Church, circa 1870	from an original photo by Rogers, from the Public Archives of Nova Scotia collection
	Little Dutch Church, steeple detail	John Lavers
4.	Barrington Meeting House	John Lavers
	Barrington Meeting House, interior	John Lavers
	Barrington Meeting House, clock	John Lavers
	Barrington Meeting House, pilaster detail	John Lavers
5.	St. George's, Sydney	George Rogers
6.	Old Holy Trinity	John Lavers
	Old Holy Trinity, chancel window	John Lavers
7.	St. Mary's, Auburn	John Lavers
	St. Mary's, door detail	John Lavers
	St. Mary's, interior	John Lavers
	St. Mary's, steeple detail	John Lavers
	St. Mary's, chancel window	John Lavers
8.	Christ Church, Karsdale	Elizabeth Pacey
	Christ Church, steeple detail	Allan Duffus
9.	Old St. Edward's, Clementsport	John Lavers
	View of Clementsport	John Lavers
	Old St. Edward's, interior	John Lavers
	Old St. Edward's, chancel window	John Lavers
	Old St. Edward's, steeple detail	John Lavers

10.	St. George's Round Church	Arthur Carter
	St. George's, view of the galleries and dome	E.G.L. Wetmore, from the Nova Scotia Museum collection
	St. George's, chancel	E.G.L. Wetmore, Nova Scotia Museum collection
	St. George's, belfry detail	Arthur Carter
	St. George's, view from the second gallery	John Lavers
11.	Old Covenanter Church, Grand Pré	John Lavers
	Old Covenanter Church, 1937	Gauvin & Gentzell, from the Nova Scotia Museum collection
	Old Covenanter Church, interior	John Lavers
	View of churchyard through the window	Allan Duffus
12.	Church of Saint John, Cornwallis	John Lavers
	Church of Saint John, south elevation	John Lavers
	Church of Saint John, door detail	John Lavers
	Church of Saint John, steeple detail	John Lavers
13.	Goat Island Baptist Church	Elizabeth Pacey
	Goat Island Church, interior	Elizabeth Pacey
14.	All Saints', Granville Centre	John Lavers
	All Saints', door detail	John Lavers
	All Saints', steeple detail	John Lavers
15.	St. Luke's, Annapolis Royal	Elizabeth Pacey
16.	Christ Church, Dartmouth	Allan Duffus
	Christ Church, interior, 1932	Gauvin & Gentzell, from the Nova Scotia Museum collection
	Christ Church, steeple detail	from the Halifax Herald collection
17.	North West Range Meeting House	Allan Duffus
	North West Range Meeting House, interior	Allan Duffus

18.	St. Mary's Basilica	Nova Scotia Information Service, 1979
	St. Mary's, steeple detail	Allan Duffus
19.	William Black Memorial Church	E.G.L. Wetmore, from the Halifax Herald collection
	William Black Memorial, 1931	A.W. Wallace, from the Nova Scotia Museum collection
20.	Cole Harbour Meeting House	Rosemary Eaton
	View of Cole Harbour	Rosemary Eaton
21.	St. Patrick's, west elevation	George Rogers
	St. Patrick's, Sydney	Brian Campbell, from the Halifax Herald collection
22.	St. John's, elevation, 1982	Elizabeth Pacey